Here's what people are saying about *Follow Your Heart*.

"If you want to find God's true purpose for your life and realize your own greatest potential, read Follow Your Heart. You will learn practical ways to turn your dreams (which are God's dreams for you) into reality. Reading this book could change your life and send you on an exciting new journey of faith."

Margaret Peale Everett
Board member, *Guideposts*; special projects participant,
Peale Center for Christian Living.

"So many of us women live a passionless life, never realizing all the potential God has put inside of us. Judy Peterson does an excellent job of identifying some of the causes for our unfulfilled lives and gives biblical advice to help us truly follow our hearts. This book will help you discover the 'good works which God prepared in advance' for you to do, and with that, to know the joy of investing your life in eternally significant activity."

Mary Whelchel,
Founder and host, *The Christian Working Woman*;
speaker, author, *If You Only Knew*

"Follow Your Heart brings memories from a long life of watching how God takes ordinary people and puts a dream into their hearts. Then, by His creative power He enables that dream to bring extraordinary accomplishment. The book is beautifully written and gives hope for all the hidden dreams."

Margaret Jensen
Author, *Papa's Place, First We Have Coffee*; speaker,
conference presenter

"As I read Judy's wonderful book, I thought back over the choices that led me to where I am now. I am struck by how often our lives only make sense in retrospect—looking at the choices, the ambitions, the tears, and (finally) the achievements. But there is another way of knowing life—seeing forward through dreams. . . . Judy's book is an invaluable tool for understanding these dreams and seeing who it is that we have the power to become."

Carolyn Rossi-Copeland
Theater producer and vice president of creative affairs,
Radio City Entertainment

Follow Your Heart

and Discover God's Dream for You

Judy Peterson

For Her. For God. For Real.
faithfulwoman.com

Faithful Woman is an imprint of
Cook Communications Ministries, Colorado Springs, Colorado 80918
Cook Communications, Paris, Ontario
Kingsway Communications, Eastbourne, England

FOLLOW YOUR HEART
© 2001 by Judy Peterson

First Printing, 2001
Printed in the United States of America

1 2 3 4 5 6 7 8 9 10 Printing/Year 05 04 03 02 01

Editor: Afton Rorvik, Julie Smith
Cover Design: Peter Schmidt
Interior Design: Peter Schmidt

Unless otherwise noted, Scripture quotations are taken from the *Holy
Bible: New International Version* ®. Copyright © 1973, 1978, 1984 by
International Bible Society. Used by permission of Zondervan Publishing
House. All rights reserved. Other Scripture quotations are taken from the
King James Version (KJV).

Library of Congress Cataloging-in-Publication Data

Peterson, Judy.
    Follow your heart and discover God's dream for you / Judy Peterson.
    p. cm.
    Includes bibliographical references.
    ISBN 0-7814-3464-5
    1.Christian women--Religious life. 2. Self realization--Religious
aspects--Christianity.
    I. Title.

    BV4527 .P42 2001
    248.8'43--dc21
                                                        00-055500

Table of Contents

Preface

This book is a result of my journey to follow my own dreams.

As you read this book, you will begin your own journey, pursuing those things that are closest to your heart. On that journey you will learn how to live purposefully as you dream about ways your talents could benefit others and honor God.

As you dream of what you could do with your life and step out in faith to act on those dreams, be assured that you will be challenged as never before, both personally and spiritually. You may have a lot of questions: *Can I really do this? What if things don't work out? How do I know if I'm doing what's best? What would God have me do?*

Personal confidence in yourself and in God become significant factors on this journey to pursue your dreams. Do you really believe God has a plan and wants good things for you? Can you discover the dream or the work God has in mind for you? These questions raise issues of faith and trust you might never have had to deal with. Your heart must search for answers.

As I asked myself these hard questions, I found myself going back to basics, particularly to God's promises and my part in their fulfillment. It was because of those promises that I found the courage to press on toward fulfilling my dreams. One of my favorite promises is,

"Delight yourself in the LORD and he will give you the desires of your heart" (Ps. 37:4). It seems almost too good to be true! (See chapter nine for other promises.)

I ultimately discovered it wasn't my own strength, wisdom, or abilities that made my dreams come true. Ironically, I remember saying once, "If I just had the chance to do something on my own, without hindrances, I could make the right things happen." How little I understood that it wasn't my own efforts, but rather God working through me that would eventually transform my dreams into reality. I just had to get out of the way.

I am sure there is much more I have to learn as I continue to follow new dreams. I only hope I can be open to the lessons in life that God has arranged for me.

Following your heart motivations and God-given dreams will involve risk and uncertainty. It will require you to trust continually in God and to persevere. I have talked with many women who express feeling "fragile" during such times. This book is written to help you in that fragile time. I want to share with you what I have learned, and what others have learned, to help you fulfill your God-given dreams. It is my hope that this book will help you in a practical way, and that it will also bolster your confidence, enabling your dreams to become a reality.

May you be granted the "desires of your heart" that God has put within you. In the process may your heart be enlarged as you share with others your services and abilities. Whether you start your own business, become a doctor, serve as a volunteer in civic or church groups, go into the arts, work at home, teach others, or help others in a myriad of ways, may you and those you serve be blessed.

Happy journeying. I wish you God's best.

TO LEN
For his constant support
and encouragement

Acknowledgments

My thanks go to the many women who graciously shared their stories with me and with the readers of this book. Such an act involved courage and trust, and I am most respectful of that. I hope these women know how much the sharing of their dreams, with all the excitement, struggles, and joy, will benefit other women, inspiring them to find God's dream, and in so doing, find truly meaningful and satisfying lives.

I also want to thank my dear friends and family for the support and the prayers they have given me. I appreciate their caring and thoughtfulness, and the many times they have asked, "How are things going?" Special thanks go to Scott and Misha, to Sheri and Keith, and especially to my husband, Len. I'm also grateful to Julie, my editor at Cook Communications, and to Linda, who gave the manuscript electronic form.

Finally, I want most of all to thank God for giving me my dreams and helping them to come true.

Chapter One

You Were Born to Dream

As Marcia sat across the table from me on the deck of one of those wonderful California restaurants that over-look the Pacific, her thoughts seemed to come and go much like the waves of the sea below. Marcia was reflect-ing on her life and wondering about her future.

"I am in my fifties. I have been working as a vice president/office manager in our family business for over fourteen years. I have been thinking about what else I could do. In some ways I feel lost—like I am not sure which way I want to go. In other ways I feel free to try new things, free to try new wings. This seems like a watershed of some kind.

"I am having a hard time deciding what to do. I know that I want to be productive. I want to make something happen, to see the results of what I do, and to be compensated for what I do. It is more important to me that I do something significant or useful than that I be successful.

"I sometimes spend a lot of time fantasizing about being in different roles, playacting in my imagination and trying on various vocations to see if I would like them. Finding the specific dream or plan is the hardest part of all. I feel that I need to be very open, sensitized to everything going on. I constantly have antennae out to hear something that will spark a response in me. Sometimes I follow a course for a while, then try something else, and finally come back to one that I had previously pursued. This makes me feel indecisive, but I know it is part of the process.

"My faith is at the root of all this. My values about what is important and why I am uniquely on this earth and in this place come from my faith. I see this time as finally the time when I can realize my potential and my goals and be fully human. Our children are launched, and our financial picture isn't going to change all that much by what I do. I like who I am. I want now to give out rather than take in. I have tons of energy most of the time and feel very poised to make a whole new beginning."

Aren't dreams strange things? They lie somewhere within us until something—a circumstance or event—suddenly causes us to remember them. Marcia, like many of us in a similar situation, became excited and hopeful as she began to consider the possibilities of making her dreams a reality. She felt it was time for her to find an activity that could bring her the satisfaction and reward for which she was looking. She went on to discuss some of her options: involvement in a training program like Stephen Covey's "Seven Basic Habits of Effective Managers," something within the selling and marketing field, or even work in conflict resolution and negotiation.

As our waiter cleared our table, I knew that with Marcia's resolve and searching, her plans would soon begin to unfold. Many of us have felt like Marcia. We may have been, or are now, at the point of either resurrecting old dreams or thinking about new dreams. Marcia wanted to do something different with her life—pursue a new dream. Such a desire can be precipitated by a change of job, an empty nest, or a fresh desire to have activities that bring meaning to our lives.

Perhaps you too are looking for a new pattern in your life and are wondering what shape your dream might take. Are you trying to incorporate activities around your role of wife and mother, or find activities that don't leave you with a "there must be more to life than this" feeling? Are you looking for better ways to use your talents, as well as better ways to integrate your family and work life? You are not alone.

Finding Balance

Louis Harris and Associates recently conducted a study entitled "Women: The New Providers" for the Families and Work Institute and the Whirlpool Foundation. This study provides the most comprehensive look at women's views about work, family, and society since 1986. It concluded that women today seek harmony between their dual roles as nurturers and providers and are not interested in shedding responsibilities as much as finding a sense of balance in their lives. Forty-eight percent of women in the survey said they would work even if money were not the concern. (The term "work" here refers to part-time work, volunteer work, or self-employment, in addition to full-time work.)[1]

Sherilyn—mother

Sherilyn, a mother in her thirties, talks about her own challenges concerning these issues.

"I've worked most of my life since I was eighteen years old. . . . Developing competency, getting professional feedback, and establishing collegial relationships in the workplace have been fulfilling for me. The past year and a half I spent finishing graduate school and not working in a job. This was the first time in many years that I hadn't worked. . . . When I finally graduated, four-and-a-half months pregnant (something I wanted), the real shock came. I quickly realized that people were not interested in hiring a pregnant woman who would soon require three months of maternity leave.

"The contrast in moving from work/school to being at home for what was to become a ten-month period was a difficult time for me. However, the ten months became meaningful to me in reevaluating my priorities as I waited for my baby to be born. I wanted to be able to address adequately my needs and those of my baby. Out of this soul-searching process came a desire to have balance. For example, the full-time work schedule I was used to would have to be tailored down to part-time hours because of my desire to be available for my baby. I am a social worker and have an understanding of the importance of the mother-child bonding process.

"There has been some loss for me because of this chosen priority, in the sense that I am not moving as fast in my professional career as I had previously wished. Since my daughter Kara's birth, however, that loss has lessened as I have a greater appreciation for motherhood and what it is teaching me. Before, I thought career plans or personal dreams would be the ultimate in terms of what defined and was important for my own development. I have been learning that career is only a portion of the pie.

"My daughter is one of the greatest things that

has arrived on my plate in life. This fooled me. I'm finding being a mother is in many ways much more deeply rewarding than my career could ever be. I don't have an obsession to get ahead, but I do have a peace that I can have some of both worlds—home and work.

"My dreams were different before my baby was born, but with her entering the world, my dreams have just taken a different shape. Some of those dreams may be delayed a bit until Kara is in school. For now I am seeking, and have found, outside part-time work activities that allow me to have the balance I think is necessary. Motherhood also creates some of that balance by forcing me to live in the present. With work one is always thinking about the future."

Exploring New Dreams or Recalling Childhood Dreams

As you think about your own life and plans, what could you see yourself doing or being? Have you thought about it? You may not be a young mother, but you may be seeking balance and purpose in your own life and wondering how to find it. Whatever stage of life you are in, most likely you desire to be productive and useful, but not at the expense of your family or yourself. It could be that for the first time, you are giving serious consideration to what you want to do with your life. You don't want to live a life of regret, of unfulfilled dreams or unused or misused skills and talents. But, as with many of us, we spend so much of life working hard and starting out in a career, having children, being busy in the home or community, or in some cases "just surviving." Time flies. Life happens while we're busy making other plans. Take the time to stop, look around, and take stock. While life may have been good for you, are there some things you just haven't had time to do? Some things you could be better at?

Popular author Jan Karon, known for her charming Mitford series that captures the heart of small town life, speaks of the time in her life when she too thought "things could be better." With just eight years of formal education, she entered advertising at the age of eighteen. In time, and after several moves, she gradually worked her way up to handling very large accounts. Yet after years of success, she felt something was missing. She explains, "I never wanted to be in advertising. It required no particular education when I went into it, just inclination and skill."[2]

At age forty-eight, Karon, feeling she could become an "old hack in the back room of a mediocre ad agency,"[3] began to pray and think of new dreams and new possibilities that would provide a heart-connection to her daily efforts. She considered her options and two years later, believing God was truly leading her, moved to Blowing Rock, North Carolina, to start a fresh chapter in her life. She had some misgivings and some fears that all this was a foolish whim, but as she sat down to write her first novel, based on ideas she had one night while lying in bed, she stated: "My heart got into it."⁴ She had found her calling. The rest, as they say, is history. Jan Karon had the faith and the courage to listen to her heart's desires, act on them, and trust God to provide direction. She has now published her fifth novel, *A New Song*, with two more in the planning stages.

While you may be in the early stages of dreaming new dreams for your own life, you may also have had dreams in your growing-up years that you have long put on hold or completely forgotten. If so, it might be time to dust those dreams off. In talking with a number of women, I have been amazed to discover how many are finding their dreams by recapturing their early desires—desires that appeared and disappeared at random over the years. Only now are they recognizing those desires for what they are and beginning to address them. These women are saying, "I always wanted to . . . I wish I had . . . or I never had the opportunity to . . ." If it is true, as many would suggest, that our mission or work is placed in our hearts by God, it should not come as a surprise that we can trace our strongest desires back to our younger years.

Eileen—author

Eileen is an example of someone who later in life returned to her original childhood dreams. Eileen is a married mother in her forties with two adopted

Korean girls. She has written and published three hundred magazine articles. Eileen attended college but didn't graduate and didn't always get the support at home in her growing-up years that she needed. Today she wants to put obstacles aside and reconnect with her long-time dream of writing books for children. She talks about her journey to accomplish this, and some of the challenges she is facing.

"Life began when I got married because I finally had independence and got away from home. I went to college, but I didn't finish. It bothers me because I was always the sterling student. However, when I was offered a good job as a reporter for a newspaper, I quit school. There is no compelling reason for me to go back to school now, but I do have some regret.

"When I was a child I loved to read. That was the most important thing in my whole life. The first time I was in a library at age six was a major event. I would check out four books at a time and read a lot about children growing up in happy homes. Characters in books impressed me so much. I said, 'I'm going to write these books some day.' Books were my escape hatch. My parents were dysfunctional. My mother was constantly creating turmoil. I didn't like it. To escape, I would live in the world of books. In the fifth grade at Catholic school I wrote a long story and kids passed it around and added to it. Writing became a big part of my life. I eventually won prizes and worked on the school paper.

"I had a friend in high school who said that I would have to pay a publisher to publish a book—thousands of dollars! I remember thinking, *No one told me this. I can't do that.* Because I believed my friend, I decided I would write for newspapers. At twenty-one I worked at a paper and won an award. Later I got a job at a small daily and did freelance work.

"I picked up my childhood dream of writing a book when my oldest daughter was nine years old. I made an effort to get it published. I got a New York agent who liked the book and received nice comments about it, but the book didn't get published. My agent gave up, and I was devastated. However, I did win a Women in Communication award that year, and that was great.

"At the point of feeling negative and doubting myself, my husband's business was embezzled. I therefore got a job working in admissions and public relations in a nursing home, with no qualifications, and worked for three years in an environment that I didn't really enjoy. Eventually my husband turned his business around, and I decided to write a book about "Prince Charming" and what I had learned in my home during those extremely difficult times. That book was published!

"I am now writing children's books again.

I really want to do this. Every time I am at a book fair I watch authors with kids standing in line in awe and say to myself, 'I want to be over there instead of being here as an author of adult books.' I gravitate to children's book authors instantly. Many such authors started late, like Madeline L'Engle and Lois Lowry, who wrote *Anastasia Krupnick*. There is hope here. I'm still in my forties!

"Money is important to me, but it is not everything. When I am writing, time just flies. You just know when you are doing the right thing. I believe if you honor what your heart is telling you, a way will be provided for you. I'm going forward with the trust that what I need will be there when I need it. I hope to finish a book soon, and I may keep doing magazine articles until I can get enough financial return to do just books.

"Choosing to follow one's heart can be the road not always taken. My best friend has a great career that is taking off. She is just blossoming and is quite glamorous. I'm still schlepping around grocery stores. I've got to get over not doing things society says are successful. My self-image gets skewed. It is easy to lose faith in yourself and your dreams, especially when friends live different kinds of lives. Fears hit the surface. . . . What if something bad happens and I gave up ways to make money? Or, I feel at times I'm the only one out there doing these things. Then, too, I think when your workplace is at home, it is easy to lose perspective or not feel professional. I have to remind myself that I am engaged in a business.

"Our dreams are a vehicle to get to where we want to go. I think being financially successful doesn't corrupt a dream. I would love to be able to say that I could support my family no matter what! I've said to God, 'I want to see my dreams fulfilled because this is what I am about. I want to be open—I'm ready to be filled up. I don't know what I need. Take me where I have to go! I don't have to orchestrate things myself.' I don't want to be shut off from the mystery. I say to God, 'Here I am. Help me, lead me, show me.'"

Eileen, in picking up on her childhood dreams, is honoring what her heart is telling her, trusting that God will provide a way for those dreams to go forward. She is learning to trust God for the results.

Following God's Leading

Most of us sometime in our lives, like Eileen or Jan Karon, have had a desire to do something. We may have had big dreams or little dreams, childhood dreams or later-life dreams, but in everyday living we downsized them. This is in no way to disparage our dreams of also being a good wife and mother—it is only to acknowledge that there are other parts of being a woman that need to be nurtured.

Wouldn't it be wonderful if, wherever you are

in your life, you could give yourself permission to consider what the dreams and plans for your life might be today? Or even more important, consider what plans and dreams God might have for you? You would not offer excuses, impose limits on yourself, or claim that extenuating circumstances seemed insurmountable. You would say instead, "I wonder if God has a dream for me—I don't seem to be using my abilities to the full." These thoughts would then lead you to consider not only your own personal dream goals but also whether you've trusted God for those goals.

You may be able to list many reasons why this might not seem like a good time to even entertain new plans or new dreams. But is there ever a perfect time? A perfect time is not when everything conspires in such an obvious way that there is no risk and opportunity falls in your lap. Rather, a perfect time is when you feel stirrings to follow dreams, a kind of inner restlessness that suggests that this is the time for a change. Such an experience is often the prodding of God. Sadly, we sometimes misread the signals and don't press forward, or we allow fear to hold us back. Hannah Whitall Smith, a Quaker author who lived in the 1800s, searched throughout her life for religious truth. She clung to the Bible's promises and found them to be as true as tempered steel. She wrote many books but was best known for the inspirational classic, *The Christian's Secret of a Happy Life*, which sold well over two million copies. In that book she writes: "If a 'leading' is of God, the way will always open for it."[5] She continues: "and when He putteth forth his own sheep, He goeth before them, and the sheep follow Him; for they know His voice." Finally, she comments: "If the Lord 'goes before' us, He will open the door for us, and we shall not need to batter down doors for ourselves. . . . His suggestions will come to us, not so much commands from the outside as desires springing up within. They will originate in our will; we shall feel as though we desired to do so and so, not as though we must."[6]

Rather than hold on to the status quo or to an outdated life pattern, you can look on your restlessness (or unhappiness) as a possible signal to move on and see what lies ahead. You can do this knowing that uncertainty and challenges will come with that decision, and that if God does have plans for you, He will start to reveal them. (Eileen certainly spoke of some of her struggles as she pursued her God-given dreams.) As you step out to follow His will, you must do so in faith.

Myths and Misconceptions of Dreaming

What could keep you from having the courage and commitment to follow a new dream? Sometimes what holds many of us back are the myths and misconceptions that we believe, or that society has perpetrated. We don't really understand what having a dream means, or we don't understand how to get in touch with our dreams. We also don't understand that God has a dream for us as women, and in particular as women of faith. So in the course of making our dreams a reality, we must dispel some myths about dreams. What exactly are some of those myths or misconceptions?

- ❦ God only has dreams for those with a great destiny.

- ❦ We will know it's God's dream, or the right dream for us, if it comes easily.

- ❦ Dreams are only for those who have the time and the luxury to pursue them.

- ❦ Dreams are only for those seeking fame and fortune.

- ❦ Having a dream is being selfish or self-centered and is contrary to God's will.

- ❦ Dreams are just for the young.

We will be addressing these myths throughout the pages of this book, often through the stories of women who are daring to dream. These women learned to disregard these myths and misconceptions and listen instead to their heart motivations.

Born to Dream

It has been said that nothing destroys the human spirit more than a lack of vision or purpose. The wisdom of Proverbs says it well: "Hope deferred makes the heart sick, but a longing fulfilled is a tree of life" (Prov. 13:12). We probably don't fully grasp that our Heavenly Father wants to see our God-given longings fulfilled. Psalm 20:4 encourages us: "May he give you the desires of your heart and make all your plans succeed." Do you really believe that God can be that involved in your life? Do I? Not always, unfortunately.

What deludes us into thinking our dreams are misplaced or in opposition to God's will? It might be fear, lack of faith, or the belief that somehow our "deepest desires" can't possibly represent God's wishes for us. (After all, doesn't God usually want us to do things we don't want to do?) Throughout this book we will be addressing your dreams in light of the fact that God does have a dream for you, and you can be a partner with Him in the fulfillment of that dream.

One of the first myths we may encounter on the way to making our dreams a reality is that following a dream is just for the famous or for those who have a great destiny. The rest of us should just settle for less, accepting our lot in life.

We must resolutely put this myth to rest because it contradicts the fact that we are made in God's image, and unlike the animal kingdom, we have the ability to imagine, to visualize, to dream, and to create. God places dreams in our hearts for a reason. Our dreams can promote His purposes for our lives and urge us to help others.

Don't we all want to believe that we have a

special gift that we can either make the world a better place or make a difference in people's lives? No matter how well we are doing, deep within us we often believe that life could be even greater. This nagging feeling is confirmed by research that states most of us use only 10 percent of our capacities in our lifetime. Many of us harbor a secret desire: "I want to contribute more."

Someone once said that true greatness is "only one inch beyond mediocrity." That inch, however, is such a great distance that we must depend on God to lead us to greatness. It is wonderful to hear everyone from athletes to mothers to movie stars accept some award by saying, "I would first like to thank God who gave me my abilities and helped make my dreams possible." History is full of people who had the courage to dream. Martin Luther King articulated his dream so forcefully in his "I have a dream" speech, moving others to action and making the world a better place.

Dreams, however, do not have to be relegated just to great thinkers. Anyone can let God dream through her and dare to do great things for God and others. True dreams, God-given dreams, are fulfilled through service by those who are willing to serve. Another myth is thus dispelled: having a dream is being selfish or self-centered and is contrary to God's will.

You were born to dream, and God can accomplish much through you as He plants them within your heart and mind. As you think about your own life and service, you can prepare to find God's dream for you by first asking, "Who am I? What are the heart motivations and abilities that God has given me?" Your answers to these questions will begin to reveal to you God's plan for your life. Then you can begin to discover your dream by asking, "Where is it I want to go? Where are my heart's desires leading me? What path should I take? What passions has God placed within me that could indicate a 'work' he has for me to do?" Once you've answered these questions, you can start to pursue your dream by asking, "How can I get to where I want to go? How can I put feet on my faith? What are the strategies and thinking that can help me to accomplish the goals I have for my life?"

In the pages to come, we will cover all of these questions, showing how they build on each other. These questions will start you on your dream-journey and also on a spiritual journey. We will also talk about the worth of pursuing a dream, including the challenges and benefits. And we will discuss the different stages of a God-given dream, what these stages mean, and your involvement in them. You may see that just when you thought your dream was dying, it really wasn't!

A Spiritual Quest

This book uses practical strategies, self-definition exercises, and inspirational principles to help you follow your dreams and heart's desires. These elements cannot be separated—all are equally important and an integral part of the journey you will be taking.

Today more and more people are seeing the value of the spiritual in the workings of everyday life, even the governing of our nation. Stephen Carter spoke of some of these issues in his book, *The Culture of Disbelief.* And Stephen Covey, respected leadership authority and author, stresses that we should continually renew ourselves physically, mentally, and spiritually. Some time ago Bill Moyers' five-part series on PBS, "The Wisdom of Faith," emphasized the part that faith plays in our lives. Clearly, many value faith in God.

When you think of your own life—who you are and where you want to go—isn't it natural to include God?

Here you will read the stories of women who are taking the journey you will be taking. They are of different ages, interests, and backgrounds, but they have all followed their heart, trusted in God, and ultimately found their dreams. These are gutsy, determined women who often had fears to overcome and challenges to face. They are no doubt just like you, and their stories are meant to provide encouragement, support, and helpful advice. Even more, I believe you will experience a bonding and shared journey with these women.

What could be more thrilling and rewarding for you than using your talents in the setting God has in mind for you and fulfilling God's purpose for you? Won't it be wonderful to find out for yourself what God might have in store for you? And to be granted your fondest heart's desires as He works through you to bring them to fruition? This is an opportunity not to be missed!

Chapter Two

Gaining the Confidence to Follow Your Heart's Desires

As you begin to take a closer look at your hopes and dreams, what would you like to do? Do you want to do something in the arts, start a business, go back to school, write a book, give seminars, or do volunteer work? Discovering the deepest desires God has planted within you can be the first step to uncovering His dreams and purposes for your life.

What Are Your Dreams?

If you could put circumstances and hindrances aside, what would your dream be for the next year or years of your life? This *if* question is a powerful tool in unlocking your hidden desires or wishes. It will free up your thinking because it feels like a game. In fact, you may be surprised at your immediate response to this question.

I posed this *if* question recently to an artist friend. My friend happens to be so talented that she has difficulty determining which of her talents she most wants to use! Pam, a parent with grown children, is trying to decide what to do at this stage in her life and what her priorities should be. When confronted with the chance to pursue her fondest desires through this *if* exercise, Pam immediately responded: "I know exactly what I would be doing. I would put on seminars that help others to use their abilities and to believe in themselves, and I would weave the topic around a book I have been working on for some time. Completing the book would be a prerequisite to doing anything else. I would then sell my art prints with inspirational themes at the seminar, but I would do my art only as a side effort and not my main focus." To Pam's surprise everything seemed to fall in place in her mind. She heard her answers to my question and realized the course of action she wanted to take.

It is amazing what happens when we brush away either real or imagined limitations and allow ourselves to really dream, with no holds barred. I have seen others like Pam, who when given the opportunity, suddenly articulate a dream that had only been a fuzzy picture. Once expressed, it began to come into focus. I think few of us fully realize how much we limit our dreams by being so tied to our present circumstances. We need to develop a greater vision of the future.

And so I ask again, what are your desires or ideas for your life? For the moment, pretend that you could follow the desires that are "springing up within," as Hannah Smith wrote. (Later you can test these dreams against Scripture, providential circumstances, inner convictions, and the leading of God.) What would you tell me about your dreams if we were sitting across a table from each other, sharing a cup of coffee? Put any thoughts you might have on a piece of paper. Don't limit your dreams. Reach beyond your present.

Also pray earnestly that God will begin to reveal His will, if He has new directions for you. Maybe you have never done this before. Maybe something always kept you from it. Our society often considers dreaming an indulgent luxury. This is another myth or misconception. Without dreams where would our society be today? How many of life's improvements, even basics, would we be missing? The electric light bulb? The automobile? Penicillin? Computers? Who would be working to discover a treatment for cancer?

Dreaming about what to do with your life and talents is foundational for doing anything, creating anything, or undertaking anything new. It should be the starting place, although we often begin elsewhere. Sometimes we let others influence us, well meaning as they might be. We start with, "I'll do what my family says to do," or "I'll go where the money is." Sometimes we also make decisions based on the head and not the heart. I have a plaque on my desk that says, "Make little decisions with your head and big decisions with your heart." It is such a wonderful reminder to stay on the heart's path. We all have heard of people who spent years in jobs or activities they did not like and were constantly trying to justify those activities. Don't be afraid to start with your dreams.

Your Meaningful Experiences

Do you know how to make the personal discoveries that are so important to your future? It begins with a look at the experiences in your life that have been especially meaningful and brought you great joy. Guidance counselors and psychologists stress that if we examine our most pleasurable and rewarding times, or achievement/experiences, we can discover an ever-present pattern of motivations and abilities, a common thread throughout our lives.

Arthur Miller and Ralph Mattson bring a Christian perspective to their work at People Management Inc. They have helped thousands of people find their individual talents and use those talents to lead productive lives. Miller and Mattson stress that "people are not only wonderfully and specifically designed, but this design remains consistent through life."[1] So when we look carefully at what we have freely willed to do over the years, our design pattern becomes obvious. We can then name the motivations and talents we have used most often. Finally, these desires and abilities can be transferred to, and incorporated in, new activities and projects. We will likely experience success in these new areas because, as Miller and Mattson explain, we will be performing the works for which we are gifted. We will be fulfilling a calling and a destiny that is from God.

Let's take a look at your life experiences, helping you to identify the desires that motivate you. This core understanding is the foundation on which you will build everything else. Your strong desires provide authenticity and staying power for whatever dream or life-work you may pursue. Someone once said that it is the strength of our purposes, not our own strength, that will sustain us during times of testing or adversity.

Don't try to document all the achievements/ experience in your life, only the peaks. They also were times when you were most yourself, doing what you wanted to do, not necessarily the times when you achieved the most. In fact, you might have been the only one aware of these peak moments. You experienced a feeling of happiness or a sense of "I don't deserve this." You felt self-directed and not influenced by others. (Unknowingly perhaps, you were following your heart.) Such experiences can be in several areas of life: school, work, church, home, hobbies, and volunteer activities. You might have been acting in a school play, leading a group at school or in the community in some kind of activity, working on a project either at work or in the home, or volunteering for something at church. Whatever the case, you can start to record the achievement/experiences that brought you much satisfaction and pleasure.

I can remember when I tried writing for the first time several years ago. I was working on my first book, *Something of Your Own,* and wondering if this was something I should really be doing. I had done a little writing in college but not professionally. I began to discover, however, that when I was writing time seemed to fly. Writing became a peak experience for me. My awareness of that experience has since guided me in making other life choices.

Your Heart's Passions

You can prepare to find God's dream for you (the desires of your heart) by first learning more about who God designed you to be. We each have different gifts according to the grace given us. What can be done with these gifts? "If it is serving, let him serve; if it is teaching, let him teach; if it is encouraging, let him encourage; if it is contributing to the needs of others, let him give generously; if it is leadership, let him govern diligently; if it is showing mercy, let him do it cheerfully" (Rom. 12:7-8).

To discover your talents and gifts, make a list of

as many of your own past or present peak experiences as you can remember. Then try to discern the motivational pattern and abilities that you drew on in these experiences. This should be an exhilarating exercise. You will definitely find something because having a pattern seems to be an absolute ingredient of how God made you. This should ease any fears about, "What if I look and I don't find anything?" You already possess a design—God's blueprint. And your design is unique. Just as God uniquely and beautifully designed each snowflake, He also created you with an intentional package of desires and talents that sets you apart from everyone else.

You will find it handy to list your peak experiences in a notebook. (This notebook can become kind of a dream-journal, as can this book.) When recording your experiences, list each one in a column, noting whether it is from school, church, work, etc. Then in a second column, describe your motivation for each experience. Finally, in a third column list the abilities you used. Look at the sample chart on page 28. Notice that a common motivation for this person was wanting to "achieve potential."

My Meaningful Experiences	My Heart Motivations/Desires	My Talents
	(What motivated me in this experience?)	(What abilities did I use?)
From school: directed school plays	encouraged others to excel, find talents, and enjoyable activities, thus achieving their potential	leadership/ communication
From work: developed a business plan and a better product	helped the business achieve its potential	marketing/strategic planning
Other experiences: (church, hobby, volunteer) leading a Bible study	desire to grow spiritually and to help others grow as well (achieve spiritual potential.	leadership/ teaching

As you think of your satisfying and meaningful experiences, list as many as you can in your note-book/journal. Begin with your early experiences, even as early as seven or eight years old. You should be able to see a motivational pattern that develops by at least your late teens.

When recalling an experience/accomplishment, don't write about feelings. Write instead about something *specific* you did, something you accomplished. For example, don't write: "I enjoyed a beautiful sunset." Write something like: "I designed and made craft items," or "I wrote a story," or "I was a group leader for a volunteer effort."

Typical Motivational Patterns

Now review your list of experiences, looking for the common motivational thrust, or *heart motivations* that were part of each of these experiences. To assist you in thinking through your motivations, take a look at some typical motivation patterns.

🍁 *Acquire/Possess—Money/Things/Status/People*
Wants to have own baby and family; wants to own toys, bicycles, houses, furniture, etc.

🍁 *Be in Charge/Command—others/things/organization*
Wants to be on top, in authority, in the saddle in order to determine how things will be done.

🍁 *Combat/Prevail—over adversaries/evil/opposing philosophies*
Wants to come against the bad guys, entrenched status quo, old technology, etc.

🍁 *Develop/Build—structures/technical things*

Wants to make something where there was nothing.

🍁 *Excel/Be the Best versus others/conventional standards*

Wants to be fastest, first, longest, earliest, or more complicated, the best.

🍁 *Exploit/Achieve Potential—situations/markets/things/people*

Sees a silk purse, a giant talent, a hot product, or a promising market before the fact.

🍁 *Gain Response/Influence Behavior—from people/through people*

Wants dogs, cats, people, and groups to react, to touch.

🍁 *Gain Recognition/Attention—from peers/public authority*

Wants to wave at the cheering crowd, appear in the newspaper, be known, dance in the spotlight.

🍁 *Improve/Make Better—self/others/work/organizations*

Wants to make what is marginal, good; what is good, better; what makes a little money, make a lot of money.

🍁 *Make the Team/Grade—established by others or system*

Gains access to the varsity, Eagle Scout rank, Silver Circle, Thirty-ninth Masonic Order, the country club, executive dining room.

🍁 *Meets Need/Fulfill Expectations—demanded/ needed/inherent*

Strives to meet specifications, shipping schedules, what the customer wants, what the boss has expressed.

🍁 *Make Work/Make Effective—things/systems/operations*

Fixes what is broken, changes what is out-of-date, redesigns what has been poorly conceived.

🍁 *Master/Perfect—subject/skill/equipment/objects*

Goes after rough edges, complete domination of a technique, total control over the variables.

🍁 *Organize/Operate—business/team/product line*

Thrives as an entrepreneur, the beginner of a new business.

🍁 *Overcome/Persevere—obstacles/handicaps/ unknown odds*

Goes after hungry tigers with a popgun, concave mountains with slippery boots.

🍁 *Pioneer/Explore—technology/cultures/ideas*
Presses through established lines, knowledge, boundaries.

🍁 *Serve/Help—people/organizations/causes*
Carries the soup, ministers to the wounded, helps those in need.

🍁 *Shape/Influence—material/policy/people*
Wants to leave a mark, to cause change, to impact.[2]

Which of these motivations might apply to you? Can you say truthfully, for example, "I was always motivated when I was *exploiting/achieving potentials.*" (When you read that sentence, substitute your own motivation, taking a cue from the preceding list.) Remember that your most rewarding experiences likely incorporated one common motivational thrust.

Discovering that motivation will hold the key to unlocking any new dreams or plans. If your motivation were to exploit/achieve potential, for example, you could consider motivational speaking or writing, developing a new product, or leading Bible study groups—any activity that had to do with developing potential.

Passions—Undefined Motivations

I have noticed an interesting phenomenon: when I hear people talking about their deepest passions (motivations, sometimes still undefined), they suddenly come alive with enthusiasm. I once saw a man literally start pounding the table. I mentioned he must be really motivated in that area of interest. (He had ideas on better ways to teach students.) Jim was unaware of the degree of his feelings and unaware he was pounding the table. I believe he gained some insights about himself in that exchange. (He later became headmaster of a school.)

Look for the topic/interest/activity that causes you to respond with increased enthusiasm. Then look for the passions/desires behind it. Motivations and passions matter because, in essence, they are what caused you to take action in the first place. Becoming aware of what inspires you can provide insights into what activities would be purposeful to you, while also fulfilling God's purposes for you.

Many of us often don't take the time to figure out what matters to us, and as a result, we live unhappy lives. Do you really know what could bring enthusiasm to your days? What would help you live life more fully? How many times have you heard someone say, "I want to find activities to be involved in, but I just don't know what excites me. I don't know what I want to do." We've all heard people say, "My heart just isn't into what I am doing now." If only these people knew what would capture their hearts, they could resolve their frustration and begin to make decisions for their lives.

A Meaning Crisis

Gail Sheehy, noted author and political journal-
ist, stresses the importance of being motivated in life
and having a passion: "The secret in the search for
meaning is to find your passion and pursue it."[3] She
talks about a Meaning Crisis and suggests looking for
one's passion: "You can start by seeing if it passes the
Time Flies test. What activity do you do where time
goes by without your even knowing it? What did you
most love to do when you were twelve years old?
Somewhere in that activity there is a hook to be found
that might pull up your dormant self."[4] Sheehy further
comments that some women find it very difficult to
define what it is they feel passionate about, especially
at age fifty or older. She claims women felt they had no
right to ask that question during the extended parental
emergency and may have deadened their imaginations
for a long time.

A Personal Exercise

When reflecting on your own passions, consider
discussing your thoughts with a friend or several
friends (or a member of your family) who are also
interested in some of these issues. Take turns asking
each other these questions:

❧ What were some of your special
achievement/experiences over the years?

❧ What did you get out of each experience?

✤ What seems to be the motivation that always inspired you in these experiences?

If you choose to do this exercise with others, do it with people whom you trust and people who *truly* care for your welfare. This creates a loving, positive, supportive environment in which people are free to give each other feedback and encouragement. You may decide to meet regularly with this group of friends and continue to do other exercises that will be presented throughout this book. (There are support groups for just about anything you can name. Wouldn't it be great to have a support group to nurture dreams—a Dream-Sharer group?)

As I think about my own life and what has always motivated me, I remember back to grade school and wanting others to realize their own uniqueness or potential. I always felt bad about one friend who didn't feel good about herself. We had many conversations together. Years later, when I was involved in businesses my husband and I had making Christmas ornaments and labels, I realized I enjoyed exploring the potentials of an idea or opportunity in business. Now I am involved in writing and speaking about how to achieve potentials, to find meaningful activities, and to follow your dreams—topics that still deal with my childhood motivation. I am sure that my own motivational pattern is "to actualize potential in people, situations, and markets."

If you are still unsure about your motivation, review your list of identity experiences. Did you list the achievements or times that truly provided satisfaction? Maybe you need to review your list.

As you continue to search for your heartfelt motivations, you can learn from the stories in this book of women who have tapped their own motivations and put them to use, each in their own unique way. Reading about these women may provide you with ideas or clues of how to look at your own interests and plans.

Gerry—doll manufacturer

Once when I was in Chicago, I came across one of the most unusual stories I have ever read. It was about a woman whose personal motivations and dissatisfaction with her career led her to start an enterprise called Heaven on Earth. Her company manufactures and markets a line of angel dolls and accompanying children's gifts, such as inspirational tapes and books. The company also gives 10 percent of its profits to charities for children around the world.

Gerry talks about why she left a six-figure dream job, trading foreign currencies for an international bank, first in Tokyo and later in New York: "I was drinking six cups of coffee before ten in the morning and going to bed with my portable phone because the markets never close. . . . At the end of the day I was really feeling, 'Is this all there is to life?' My parents taught me there has got to be a way that I can contribute and give back. . . . I thought, *Wouldn't it be nice if at the end of the day I felt I was spiritually enhancing myself or others?* . . . I felt this tremendous calling to do something."[5]

In the meantime Gerry's father, a doctor, became critically ill. Gerry took a trip to Bosnia, delivering medical supplies from her father, and spent weeks in the harsh winter working with local charities that care for abandoned children. When she returned home, she knew her life had changed. She was greatly moved by the terrible destruction she witnessed and by her father's now terminal illness. Gerry explains, "This gave me the determination to make my life as worthwhile as possible because I realized how fleeting it is. I really wanted to start a business doing something for children."[6]

Gerry found her dream for her life by following her heart. Is she happy with her decision? She claims: "It's what you do with what you're given that counts. . . . I am happiest when I am giving to someone else, and when I'm holding a little baby in an orphanage." In summary, she says, "I love to dream . . . in ten years, Heaven on Earth will be—to use the positive—an international company. We will have dolls of every race and nationality. We will support global charities. We will have a successful mail order catalog that is international, and we will have a retail chain where children can come in and play in our stores." And finally Gerry's goal is "to have more time to go around to the different charities and help, not just by giving money but by giving of my own time because that is where I derive a lot of self-fulfillment."[7]

Gerry's story is a great example of someone who started a venture that incorporated her strongest motivations and concerns. And what a story it is! It shows so graphically how one's heart's desires can be the springboard for a dream, a dream that can turn into a business, activity, or calling with unlimited opportunity.

Gena—doctor

When Gena speaks, she definitely stands out from the crowd. She clearly communicates her drive for excellence as well as her courage to press on, regardless of circumstances. It wasn't a life of ease that allowed her to pursue her dream and passion of becoming a doctor. She had to work hard and overcame several hurdles. This African-American woman is truly remarkable.

"I'm a radiologist, and I have been doing a fellowship for a year at the Faulkner-Sagoff Center (Boston) for breast health care.

"I never really thought that I wouldn't be a doctor, even as a child. It seemed crazy to consider. My parents gave encouragement to me; my father had only a sixth grade education, and my mother finished high school. For economic and racial reasons my father had to cut his schooling short. But my parents always said, 'You can do whatever you want to do. . . .'

"I really never considered that I would not go to medical school or that it wouldn't happen. However, it would not have happened without divine intervention. There were others who noticed and helped me along the way. My mother again encouraged me to 'work hard and someone will always be there to help you reach your goals. Be prepared, and don't worry how things will happen.'

"I had a choice of private schools for high school and college, with scholarships, otherwise that would not have been possible. . . .

"The big challenge for me was freshman chemistry in college. I thought, *This isn't going to work—if this is my dream, this shouldn't be so difficult.* I failed chemistry on my first mid-term. This made me start thinking that I would go into psychology, and I altered my dream. . . . I remember praying much in my freshman year to be at peace with my newfound direction. Every day was so painful. I finally prayed a prayer of surrender. . . . Then in spring of my sophomore year in college, I was awakened with the brightest sunlight in my room. I woke up spontaneously with a burning passion to be in medicine. It felt like a calling. After that I never gave up on my dream again. That morning was a confirmation to me that it was more than a dream I wanted; it was something I had to do. If I hadn't had that confirmation, I think I would have given up on my dream. There certainly were obstacles after that, and without confirmation, I might have doubted this was meant to be.

"One big obstacle for me is financial. I had to borrow much money to get through medical school, and I have huge expenses. Another obstacle is racism. It is ever present, and was in medical school and in my residency. Sometimes it is subtle, and sometimes not so subtle. It's my daily prayer not to be affected by that, but it is a reality.

"I am older than some are in my pursuits because I took time off between college and medical school. I taught high school and junior high for one-and-a-half years as a substitute teacher. Sometimes I wonder if that break made me lose some stamina. If I were younger, would it have been easier? I'm in my late thirties now. Maybe age was actually an advantage.

"I entered the fellowship program in breast imaging upon completion of my residency. Right now I feel very useful where I am. I feel like I've found my niche, and I serve a useful purpose. . . . I've learned to rest and let God direct me, not to be so worried how things will turn out. I cannot make all the right decisions by myself. I need God's guidance daily. I'm not nearly as fearful as I was ten years ago, and I don't have to know every detail of my dream.

"We have to prepare ourselves and not sit and wait for answers. But we have to have faith while we are working that we will be directed in the right way. As I look back, I see myself riding along, steered and guided as on a journey. Sometimes it is hard to know when I have done enough and should stop trying and let God direct me. But I don't want to do everything in my own strength.

"It is great to be at Sagoff and hear many say, 'I am so happy to see you here taking care of me.' I know some black women see me where I am and are encouraged. I'm there to serve anybody who needs my services, but it is especially gratifying to serve those who feel maybe no one can identify with them. I consider it a privilege to use my expertise to help others, and I consider it a privilege to be a physician!"

Gena dispels the myth that dreams are only for people who have the time or the luxury to follow a dream. While Gena had her share of unpleasant obstacles, they helped to sharpen her focus and fuel her commitment.

I would say that both Gena and Gerry had the

same primary motivation—to serve and to help. Gerry was also motivated to organize and be an entrepreneur. Each of these women followed her heart and in doing so discovered a dream/work that could benefit others.

Lisa—caregiver

Lisa lives in the Midwest, and is married with two older children. She provides care for the elderly. She calls on those in nursing homes and private homes, doing everything from writing letters, reading stories, to running errands. . . . If this weren't enough, Lisa also has taken in foster babies, keeping them until they could be placed in appropriate homes.

I asked Lisa what keeps her going. She replied that she is the happiest when "I am serving or helping others." It is obvious that Lisa's motivational pattern is to serve/help, and she has incorporated that desire into worthwhile activities of her choosing, activities that work around her being a mother with her own children to care for.

Your Strongest Motivation

Have you identified the heart motivations that are part of your design and can give birth to your own dreams? Remember, these motivations don't have to lead to starting a business or to becoming a doctor. They can be used in a variety of ways. Don't feel that you must immediately make a life-changing decision.

Right now, just try to figure out what interests you most, as Gerry, Gena, and Lisa did.

If you haven't done so yet, write your strongest heart's desires in your notebook/journal. You can also record it here.

My strongest motivation or passion is to:

_____

_____

_____.

(Refer back to the list of motivations on page 29.)

What abilities do you possess that can help further the desire expressed above? Imagine not being able to do anything about it. This would be a cruel trick of fate. If you've done a good job of finding your true heart motivations, however, this needn't happen to you.

In the next chapter when you go to your so-called talent/tool bag, you should discover the resources to fulfill those desires. God made no mistakes when He gave you the gifts and abilities He did. They are within you for a reason. They will be a critical part of any lifework you pursue. God may already be preparing and leading you toward the "good works" that He has prepared in advance for you to do.

Chapter Three

Letting Your God-Given Talents Lead

Discovering your passions and talents can be a life transforming experience, enabling you to wholeheartedly give to others. This discovery can provide direction for a career path and also lead you to activities that are compatible with who you are. What a difference when your gifts match your tasks!

Before embarking on the dream-activity that embraces your heart's natural motivations, you need to understand the talents that can assist in implementing that activity. The more aware you are of them, the easier it will be to evaluate the reality of your dreams and goals. As you discern the abilities God has given you, you will also begin to discern God's will for your life.

What Are Your Talents?

In chapter two we talked about listing your achievement/experiences, motivations, and abilities/ talents in three separate columns. Now, go back and look at the list of these experiences and ask yourself: *What abilities/talents did I use in each of these experiences?*

If you are doing this exercise with a friend, take turns asking each other this question. I have used this approach when giving seminars and found that partners in this exercise can greatly help each other recognize talents that were part of an experience or achievement. They can point out talents or skills that were often overlooked. For example a partner might say: "Jill, I keep hearing you say you were always putting things in order and seeing that things were done in a timely way. Do you realize that it is a talent you frequently used? In business that talent would be called organization. Whether used in the home, church group, or business it is the same ability. You have organizational skills." It is exciting to see people recognize a talent they didn't know they had. They are never the same. That knowledge alone becomes a strength and a factor in personal growth.

While discovering a talent/skill at any age is wonderful, it seems especially rewarding a little later in life. Such a discovery is like an unexpected gift. Some of the stories you will be reading in this book are about women who made such a discovery in their fifties, or even older. When they embraced this discovery wholeheartedly, they understood themselves in a new way and found the courage to pursue new dreams. This book also contains stories of women with children at home who invested their talents in activities compatible with motherhood. These activities may point the way to future undertakings when the children are grown.

Michelle—artist, writer, teacher, actress

Michelle's story is an example of a woman who incorporated her talents with motherhood. She used her ability in the arts throughout her life, but recently she has begun to see her abilities in a new light. All along Michelle let her talents lead the way, but it took time, confidence, awareness, and support of others for those talents to express themselves freely. It seems to take time for many of us to learn who God made us to be—and that understanding continues over a lifetime.

"I've always loved being around children and always loved art and drama. I hadn't been able to recognize that as a gift from God until I saw the response of children and others around me. They encouraged my teaching skills and abilities on the stage and with a paint brush. I gradually began to understand these were God-given talents and that what I loved to do is what God has called me to do.

"What I love most is to be an influence and to encourage others. The first inkling of that came in high school when I was given a role in a play, had a piece of art noticed, or had a child run up to me and hug me for no apparent reason.

"It took me a while to realize that my heart's desires, not the desires of my parents who wanted me to become a doctor, were more than enough and a delight for me.

"Upon graduating from high school I first attended Rice University and then graduate school at Harvard, taking teaching courses. I was involved in numerous college and semi-professional theater productions, my favorites being *Fiddler on the Roof* and *Godspell.* I never thought I was great, but people around me did.

"After graduate school, I found an appreciative audience for my art work as an elementary school teacher. The kids thought I could draw marvelously, even though I often thought they could draw better than I could! This encouragement, however, led me to write and illustrate my first children's book, which I am still working on getting published.

"Twelve years later I find myself continuing to be involved in art and drama, but with some different twists. I have been gleefully married to a wonderful man named Scott for ten years and have two delightful children. Sasha is in first grade and Noah a third grader at Covenant School, a Christian school in Massachusetts.

"I am now finding myself balancing mother-hood with several activities—school pickups, soc-cer games, ballet classes, Little League, and also a great desire to work with other children. At Covenant School, I'm teaching creative writing and Bible class to fifth and sixth graders three days a week, teach-ing an advanced acting class to the middle school-ers, and codirecting and producing the annual school play.

"It sounds like a lot to juggle, but God has graciously allowed me to fulfill my heart's desires so somehow it's a delight and easy to work with my own and other kids. I may not have as much energy as I did in my college years, but I believe I have creativ-ity to use in many ways. With the help of a godly husband, a supportive church and school environ-ment, and lots of pasta for dinner, I'm somehow able to keep doing the things I love.

"When all my energy is spent by being a good listener and supportive teacher, Scott will often take over for me, feeding us all and putting us all to bed. Our children do love seeing their mama at school, and they enjoy hearing the other children sing my praises.

"Through having my own children and through believing in myself enough to use my gifts, I am beginning to see God's faithfulness and love for me and also see myself as God sees me. I look at myself not only as an actress and an artist, but most important as a teacher and an encourager. My greatest joy is allowing children also to see themselves as God sees them.

"I would say to women, 'Follow what you love to do, your passion, and God will be faithful in giving you all you need. Even when you have young children, God will allow you to pursue your dreams in some fashion, perhaps more scaled down than you'd like. But children grow oh-so-fast and our time with them is the most precious gift of all.'

"Right now it feels like I'm taking baby steps toward my possible lofty goals of being more involved as an artist, writer, and actress, while still being involved with kids and school. But I always want to be careful to follow God's path for my life wherever He leads."

In reading Michelle's story, we see her growing in awareness of her talents as she used them and as she received feedback from those around her. She is going to build on that knowledge, I am sure. I would not at all be surprised to hear that in a few years, when her children are older, Michelle is busy in community theater or directing and producing programs, possibly for cable TV. Whatever she does, Michelle is blossoming and becoming the person God made her to be.

Recognize Specific Talents

It is important to realize that age isn't a barrier to using our talents, and that God would have us use our talents and gifts throughout our lifetime. This is not a matter of seeking self-fulfillment; it is a matter of stewardship of the resources God has so richly bestowed upon us as we are to "bear fruit in every good work."

Ask God to help you see the talents and potential He has given you. Later you can ask Him to give you creative ideas about how to use them. While the exercises in this book are meant to help you, they do not replace the divine leading and the enlightenment that God alone can give.

As you begin to think about the talents corresponding with your achievement/experiences from work, school, home, etc., refer to column three on your chart in chapter two, or refer to your notebook. In looking at these experiences and reviewing them, you should notice four to six abilities that recur in at least half of your achievements. To assist you in thinking through and identifying those abilities, here is a list of examples:

Administer/Maintain
Analyze/Evaluate
Build/Develop
Control/Schedule
Convince/Persuade
Create/Shape
Design/Draw
Do/Execute

Formulate/Theorize
Innovate/Improvise
Innovate/Improvise
Learn/Study
Make Friends/Build
    Relationships
Nurture/Nurse
Observe/Comprehend

Operate/Run
Organize
Perform/Entertain/Be a Showman
Plan
Practice/Perfect
Research/Experiment
Synthesize/Harmonize
Teach/Train
Write/Communicate [1]

You might not give your abilities these particular titles, but seeing these descriptions may help you to recognize abilities from your own experiences. The key is to determine the categories that were central in your accomplishments.

Here are some examples of how to look for abilities. Let's say you have the ability to convince and persuade. You might say: *I was always demonstrating leadership with others, even as a child. I remember that when I was only five I always persuaded my friends to do what I wanted to do. As I got older, I often convinced others to do something they were unsure of doing or helped them to make decisions. I also used this ability in a sales job I had, in which I sold cosmetics.*

Or maybe you have the ability to manipulate/motivate. You might say: *I could get people to come around to my way of thinking and could motivate them to take action. I remember being a group leader at school. Later at work, I was responsible for getting others to take part in a training program and a course that would benefit them. Some resisted, but eventually were motivated to go ahead. I got great satisfaction in doing this, and many later thanked me.*

Now, review your peak experiences, referring to the list of talents in this chapter, and write a statement summarizing your preferred or most used talents. Do this both here and in your journal. (Or, read the stories that follow for help in seeing your own talents and then write down your thoughts. Limit the number of abilities you list to no more than seven categories or groupings. You should see the same talent listed several times.)

My best talents and resources are:

_____

_____

_____

_____

_____

_____

_____

_____

_____

_____

_____

Women have been accused of selling themselves short or not knowing what they are good at. I happen to know someone who organizes everything and everybody, but when a friend told her that she has organizational skills, she replied: "Doesn't everyone do this?" Sometimes we overlook or take for granted what comes easily to us.

You can gain so much by naming your abilities. And your limitations. In other words, your greatest weakness is not knowing your strengths and your greatest strength is knowing your weaknesses.

I must add here that I don't believe in trying to make weaknesses stronger; I believe in building on strengths. The first approach is an uphill battle and a mistake. Did you ever repeatedly ask someone to do something, only to discover it didn't come naturally to that person and he or she simply couldn't do it? It is a myth that we are good at doing all things. Sadly, this myth has been perpetuated by business leaders who are good in some areas but act as if they are good in all. Many consider it a weakness to acknowledge anything else. I don't agree. I think it is a strength to acknowledge what you do well and to surround yourself with those who compliment your own abilities *and* limitations.

Mary Ellen—storyteller

As I think of someone who came to realize the abilities and talents she had a little later in life and put them to use in an unusual way, I think of Mary Ellen. I met Mary Ellen when my husband and I were about to give a party in a barn and were looking for entertainment. We wanted to have something different so I came up with the idea of getting a storyteller. Someone suggested I contact Mary Ellen, which I did. The result was a wonderful evening for our guests. Mary Ellen later told me about how she came to be a storyteller.

"In high school I started to be more aware of some things I wanted to do. Unfortunately, as a young woman, I was pushed into certain areas, such as teaching, nursing, or marriage. If I wanted to do anything else, I was discouraged.

"In my English class my teacher introduced me to Shakespeare. We studied plays and went to see *The Taming of the Shrew*. It was so amazing for me to see that and experience literature come to life. I felt inside me I would love to write and to allow my creative part to come out. I would love to put ideas on paper that could touch many people. Yet, because it was a time of conservatism, again I was not encouraged to pursue those types of things. They were okay in class.

"I put the part of me that wanted to write and express my feelings into hobbies. I took dance classes, some art classes, and music lessons. Still, though I enjoyed all I did, something was not fulfilled in me.

"Then I saw my first professional storyteller at a convention I was attending. For forty-five minutes she held us spellbound with her stories. I turned to the person I was with and said, "I want to do that." I had no doubts! It was a defining moment, just as when I saw the Shakespeare play. It took me a while (about four years) to find someone who could teach me how to be a professional storyteller. Finally, I got into a class and had a superb teacher.

"Today I am storyteller part time and work in an office part time. I would like to be doing storytelling full time. Sometimes I feel divided because when I'm at the office I keep thinking I could be working on a story or making phone calls to get bookings. But when I am starting out on something I need to have some kind of security, namely, a paycheck.

"Starting something new is very risky. There is a tendency to always second-guess yourself, even though your gut tells you to follow your dream. I hope I can gradually drop my part-time job as my dream becomes more stable, but in the meantime I still have to buy food and meet my expenses. I figure out how much I need to survive per month and how many hours of work I need to do that. That is all the time I'm willing to work at a part-time job.

"When you have a dream, you need to be introspective and take a practical look at what is essential for daily survival. You need to come to the

point of saying, 'I know what I need to survive physically. I can take the risk.' It must be a conscious
decision. You also need to have a sense of urgency:
'I have to do this now!'

"In the past year I have been trying to work out
my life's path. I was offered the chance to work full
time but made the choice to stay working part time
and continue as a storyteller. I also made a decision
to go to graduate school for a master of arts in literature and writing. This is my new dream.

"I am motivated to make a difference in someone's life and to be of service. This doesn't have to
be a major thing. I don't have to end up on television.

"When pursuing a dream, I believe you have to
ask yourself, 'What is important to me personally?'
Then you must take a risk. Those who don't take
such a risk will always be missing something."

It is interesting to see how Mary Ellen was
sensitive to her own desires, talents, and "defining
moments" in her life (peak experiences). She eventually took that knowledge of herself and her ability to
write, speak, communicate, and entertain/perform and
found an activity that allows for all. She is immensely
pleased with her storytelling and the satisfaction it
brings to herself and many others. I was impressed that
Mary Ellen approached her dream with a keen sense of
reality and goal setting—making sacrifices to have a

job and to go back to school—while not sacrificing her heart's desires. Everything she is doing takes her a step closer to making her dreams come true.

By now you are identifying interests and gaining insights about your own abilities. If true to your motivational pattern and talents, you too can dream of a "work" that will be meaningful, a "dream-work" fulfilling God's calling for you.

It is not self-serving to think of how you could put your abilities to use in effective ways. 1 Peter 4:10 tells us: "Each one should use whatever gift he has received to serve others." In the pages ahead you will be looking at how you can use your talents to provide a worthwhile service of benefit to others.

Andrea—artist

Andrea is a woman who knows her talents and has started to think about her dreams. But she must also face some fears as she thinks about all she may be called upon to do.

"I have always known that I have creative ability. Some things are so natural you assume everyone has them. I used to go for Sunday drives with my parents and "re-do" houses as we passed by. I also knew I was organized and found out when I took a logic course that I was very methodical. I do find I am happiest when I am creative *and* organized. I also love to know everything—what others are doing, and what is going on.

"When I was younger and had children at home, I started to wonder what else I could do with my life. I ended up getting together with twelve women, and we decided to have antique sales twice a year. During the year we would hunt, buy, and refinish these antiques. Our sale became the social event of the season—everyone came! After a while I decided there was no color at our sales—all was wood. Everyone looked at me and said: 'Why don't you start painting some things?' I started hand painting metal trunks, tin boxes, antique stoves, trays, and mirrors. I did this all during my children's growing-up years. I could work at home and take trips to look for furniture everywhere! Later on I did handpainted baskets. That evolved into painting for decorators, doing custom orders for mirrors, dressers, chairs, and so on. I even had my own studio.

"Now that my children are grown up, I have some other ideas. I would like to do hand painting on upscale clothing, such as coats and blazers. It will be nice not to have to haul heavy furniture around like I used to do in my antique business.

"Eventually it would be fun to do special things, such as scenes of one's favorite vacation place. Doing custom work makes an item so personal and unique. . . . I am excited about these ideas. Now I have to ward off fear. This all is scary for me. The ideas are easy, but the execution—the 'how to'—has me baffled. Where do I start? How do I market? Where do I get the clothes? Sometimes for some women, especially those of us who didn't have a lot of affirmation from parents, fighting old self-tapes from the past and marching forward is challenging. We need to keep saying, 'We can do it!' Sometimes we wonder if we can.

"I think a lot of women doubt themselves during the 'how do I go about it?' stage. The first step is the hardest when you're not sure. With the second step you gain momentum. It's important to keep being convinced that you will succeed. I try to be sure that my reality is not someone else's reality. Other people might not have my passions, and I don't want to live life in reaction to others, or others' rejections of my dreams. Rejection can always be hard, but I would say to other women, 'Go for it.'"

As you take steps to follow your own dreams and to use your talents, you may hit times filled with anxiety, just as Andrea did. Andrea believes the time when one begins to carry out a dream-idea is the time of most self-doubt. To do new things is to leave comfort zones and to try the unknown. But, as Andrea pointed out, it is important to keep believing you will succeed.

Since I talked with Andrea, she has gone back to school and finished college, majoring in art. She also has opened a store in Kennebunkport, Maine, called Carrots, where she will display some of her artistic endeavors and selections. And most recently, she opened a sister Carrots store in Portland, Maine. She is a lady on the go, and the momentum she has gained in following her dreams has helped carry her forward. She has gradually left her fears behind. Now she is moving mountains! She is a very gifted lady, not only using her skills as an artist, but also her organizational and leadership skills. How else would she accomplish so much in such a relatively short time?

Carolyn—producer

And there is Carolyn. Carolyn was the founding director of the Lamb's Theater Company in New York City. The company sought to discover, develop, and produce plays that explore important personal and social issues and that stress positive values. Carolyn acted as director for over seventeen seasons. She produced more than sixty off-Broadway plays and musicals. She also directed a Christmas celebration in Minsk, Belarus, in conjunction with CitiHope International and the Pioneer Children's Palace of Belarus. In addition she produced several national tours of musicals. Carolyn is someone who adamantly believes in finding one's passion and gifts. Her own unusual things that she had not planned on doing. That can be the surprise element in a dream's journey.

"I went to Tulane University and got a graduate degree in political science. Before I came to New York, I worked on Capitol Hill for Congressman Peter Rodino, Jr., for two years. It was an exciting time for a twenty-two year old. Women were being real contributors and were in great positions of responsibility. I wrote the congressman's speeches and booked all of his appointments to academies. I loved what I was doing and what I was trained to do. But every night I was involved in community theaters, directing, acting, and doing choreography. It was in me. When Congressman Rodino saw my picture in *Washington Magazine,* he asked me what I really wanted to do with my life. He said, 'Why not give it a try in the theater?'

"I left the Hill and went on a tour, working around the country in the dinner theater circuit. My parents were mortified. My dad was an immigrant from Italy and a diplomat. He thought I wanted to be a chorus girl! However, he died in 1984, and in his briefcase was a file with all of my reviews.

"I eventually met a young man on my tour who was a devout Christian. He gave me a Bible and showed me life could be more real—what I did could be pertinent. He knew about the Lamb's in New York City. The Lamb's had had a ministry in Times Square for several years at that time. My friend wanted to be a part of that ministry. I was already doing professional theater in the city and so

I went to the pastor of the church that was housed there and asked if I could rent the theater (in the building) to produce a tour. He said yes and I produced a tour that went to the Virgin Islands. It was my first venture as a producer.

"After I came back the pastor asked me if I would like to start an official theater company at the Lamb's. Days later I said, 'I'd love to do it. But I don't want to start a theater surrounded just by Christians.' He gave me his blessing, and the Lamb's Theater Company was founded in 1978. It was legitimate, off-Broadway, with all kinds of plays produced in keeping with Judeo-Christian values. For instance, in *Painting Churches* we dealt with the question: 'What have you done that has cost you something?' The Lamb's Theater became a thriving, truly Christian-in-spirit community.

"I have a continuing passion to create a theater experience that evolves into a new community for each person, rich or poor. People are given the opportunity to learn something about each other. *Godspell*, for example, offered a great opportunity to do that.

"I have always loved the theater and organizing kids and people into an event—doing a pageant, putting on a show. I am very 'event' oriented. And I am passionate about things of spirit and the theater. I have also had a women's Bible study and prayer group that is held in the governor's mansion in Albany. I wouldn't cut it at IBM!

"I think the greater the risk, the greater the chance for fulfillment. When I started out, I had no pension and no health plan. I would rather be poor and work at what I love. All gifts come from God. I am giving my gift and don't want to hide my light under a bushel. When I started I had talent, but God is multiplying it now. I am uncomfortable with praise because it is not for me. It is for what God has given me.

"I am going to be leaving the Lamb's Theater, and I have been asked to supervise a production of *Mary and Joseph* at Madison Square Garden. I have been working on it for a long time, and I am also working on some other projects. Some time ago I went to Minsk and created and directed a production involving seventy-four Russian kids. Every year I start wondering what I can do that was not planned. Some opportunities are for pay, and some are not. I must take on projects! I'm going to go and just do it!

"I have four daughters, and I try to ignite them and give them a passion. I would like them to set simple goals. I tell them what I am doing is God's gift to me. I would never have chosen the life I have and probably would have chosen a less full life. But life is so much better than if I had chosen the one I thought I wanted. . . .

"I think whatever stage a woman is at, whether

a mom or at the start of a career, she can find a way to use her passion somewhere, perhaps in the community as a volunteer or to mentor younger children. You, too, can be an example, with whatever gift you have, and do what you can. If you have kids, give to that group. God rewards what you do, even the smallest thing."

It is interesting to see how Carolyn's political science background and her work on Capitol Hill, while enjoyable, did not represent her strongest passions or where she wanted to use her talents. She pursued her love of "things of the spirit and theater" and her ability to organize "kids and people into an event" by first doing volunteer work in the theater—and that love eventually led her to Madison Square Garden! Who would have guessed that would happen?

Carolyn is a very pro-active person with faith in God. Her story clearly displays her ability to take initiative in whatever she does. It may give you ideas about definitive steps you can take in getting "out there" yourself and doing whatever you most enjoy doing. Sometimes just in the doing, or volunteering as Carolyn did, other things begin to happen. It can be a combination of learning as you go and being in the right place at the right time. This only takes place, however, when your light isn't hidden under a bushel.

Well, where are you now? You have taken a look at *who you are* in preparing for your dreams, and you are ready to turn your thoughts to discover the dream that can take advantage of the abilities and passions God has given you. You may not dream of becoming a doctor, a Broadway producer, an artist, or a manufacturer of angel dolls. What is your dream? Whatever it is, it's to be cherished because when your dream is God-directed, you can accomplish far more than you could ever imagine. How wonderful, too, that you don't have to covet the dreams of others, because you know God has special things in mind just for you.

Chapter Four

Finding the Dream God Gave You

To have a dream is the first step toward making that dream a reality. If you don't have a dream, as the popular play *South Pacific* exclaimed, "how are you going to have a dream come true?" What makes the difference between finding your dream or not finding it? Searching for it with all your heart is a determining factor, as is believing you have the resources to turn your dream into reality and also truly believing that God has a "work" for you to do.

You can start to discover your dream by asking yourself this question: *What direction or path would my heart's interests suggest?*

Where Do You Want to Go?

Let's examine some of the choices that are available to you as a woman. John Naisbitt and Patricia Aburdene coauthored a book, *Megatrends for Women,* in which they talk specifically about ten opportunities as the twenty-first century begins. According to these authors, here are the top options for women in the new century. (I'd like to keep number one a surprise for the moment.)

2. CEO/Entrepreneur
3. Health Care
4. Finance
5. Traditional Jobs Revisited
6. High Tech/Science
7. Food, Glorious Food
8. The Professions
9. Traditionally Male-Dominated Occupations
10. The Arts and Media

Naisbitt and Aburdene claim that they arrived at these "hot jobs," by asking: "How many accountants, surgeons, or teachers will the economy need by, say, 2010?" But, the authors also issue this warning: "Don't get too carried away with society's needs. What about your needs, talents, and desires for creative self-expression?" *Opportunity number one,* according to the *Megatrends* authors, *is to follow your dream:* "If your dream job is fashion designer, anchorwoman, or U.S.

senator, what do you care what the 'high growth jobs' are?"[1] They continue: "In the practical matter of choosing one's work, we believe the best advice is to follow your heart and be 'impractical.' People who love their work have a better chance at success."[2]

This is most unusual. Aburdene and Naisbitt have been respected forecasters since the publication of their original bestseller, *Megatrends*. Now they are telling women, despite all their advice about "hot jobs," what matters most is following your own dream and your own heart. Yes, there are many opportunities available, but being aware of your heart's strongest desires will lead you to the best opportunity.

It is not easy to follow your dream, as Aburdene and Naisbitt suggest. It is much easier to get caught up in what others or society would tempt you to do. For many reasons, we are all tempted to ignore the voice of our heart and the voice of our God. One reason may be that someone discouraged our dreams when we were young. Often this dream-killer only used two simple words: "Be realistic!" Having someone say, "Be realistic!" is like having an archer shoot an arrow into a balloon. This very thing happened to a friend of mine. I watched this woman describe her dreams, and then I also watched a well-meaning family member shoot it down by saying, "Be realistic!" My friend quickly packed her dream back in a box within her heart and slammed the lid shut. I have never heard her talk about it again.

Another reason we sometimes don't follow our dreams is that we listen too much to the voice of logic: "You can't do this. You have never done this before." Or, "Why do you think you can do this? Look at your circumstances." The Bible contains several stories of people whom God chose to do something special and who had many excuses why they could not. (We'll hear more of that later.)

Following Your Heart's Path

I would like to ask you, as you reflect on the thoughts you have had while reading this book, to expand your dream. Temporarily set aside anything that could inhibit that dream, such as logic or circumstances. You are about to engage in a forbidden activity—daydreaming. Why do I say forbidden? Because many of us consider daydreaming frivolous. Taking the time to suspend hindrances to what you desire for your future, however, can be an effective way to test and sound out your ideas and plans. This exercise will allow your dreams to surface. It will also let your dreams "breathe," to see if they can develop a life of their own. You are giving yourself permission to dream.

To help you decide on the dream you would like to pursue, begin by enlarging on what you think your various options might be. You could think about the opportunities that *Megatrends* mentioned, as long as you examine them from the vantage point of your own heart motivations. You could consider other opportunities as well. We have already heard from an author, a storyteller, a producer, and a teacher. You could also think about service opportunities within your community, church, or school. These may be done part time or full time, as a paid worker or as an unpaid worker. What matters most is where your passions and abilities lie.

I would encourage you to take some quality, quiet time right now. Prayerfully begin to exercise your imagination. In chapters two and three you learned what motivates you and what abilities are yours—in essence who you are. Now, begin to think about what you could do as you incorporate your motivational pattern and talents in your "work." In other words, ask yourself: "What would I be doing if I were doing what motivates me most, while using my best talents?"

Perhaps with eyes closed, picture yourself doing several things, each time changing the setting and the activity. Write down several dream activities as they occur to you, no matter how unusual. (Your list can also include the embryonic dreams you wrote down in chapter one.) Ask God again to enliven your heart and mind and to begin to show you the dream He has for you. Remember that this desire will spring from within you, most often in the form of a creative idea or vision. (As I have mentioned earlier, your desire to do something new can be God's way of prodding you out of your comfort zone and nudging you into greater things—God's choices for you.)

Where can you join God in a work or service He has for you?

Be alert for that dream. It will be the dream that you will not be able to let go because once you make yourself available to God, He will begin to lead you and "stir up" your mind and heart.

The purpose of this daydreaming exercise is for you to get in touch with your choices. Some of those choices—probably one in particular—will start to stand out.

Here are some questions you can ask yourself as you make your list.

* What activities or opportunity would incorporate my specific talents and heart motivations?

* Who could benefit from my fulfilled dream?

* Where would I serve?

* How would I serve?

* Does this activity excite me more than others, even though I have never done it and it challenges me?

* Does this activity spring from the strong desires I feel God has planted in me?

As you answer these questions, you will notice that the "what" question starts to answer "who" could be interested, the "who" question starts to answer "where" you can find an opportunity, the "where" question starts to tell what you have to do to reach those you'd like to serve, and the "how" question highlights the best way to provide your "service." You will discover that each of these questions could also raise many other questions as you put together the framework for your dream-opportunity.

By answering all of these questions, your dream gradually begins to take shape. You can then look at your answers and findings and ask: *Is this idea or dream one that I could find worthwhile and one that I could commit to? Will this dream allow God to use me and my talents?* As I've said before, God wouldn't ask you to do anything incompatible with your stage of life or incompatible with your standards and talents. He will, however, ensure that you depend on Him for your dream's fulfillment.

What you most love to do, or what reaches out and engages you, is a strong indicator of what you have the potential to become. For now, don't dismiss any ideas as impossible. The only criteria at this moment is that you listen to the desires and motivations God has brought to your attention.

I went through some of these exercises after selling a business that my husband and I had in the '80s—a Christmas ornament company. Because our primary business was a label company, we also had a business marketing designer Christmas ornaments, using a label on a glass ball, similar to Hallmark's ornaments. When our interests changed, and we decided to sell the ornament business, I found myself wondering what to do with my life. I had been actively involved in the ornament company and had no desire to be involved in the label company, which we still had. Because our two children were grown up and no longer living at home, I knew I had to have something to do. But what? I wanted answers—God's answers.

I pictured myself doing different activities, some more familiar because of my business background. This was the first time I had taken such a hard look at myself and at what God might have in store for me. I, like you, "tried on" several dreams and made a list of each of them. I could see that some dreams appealed to me a lot more than others. Even though in each dream I was incorporating my own motivations, one dream really stood out: to write about how women could find their unique gifts and also find meaningful work and lives, as well as a stronger faith and trust in God for their future.

I'd like to say that if I had approached my dream logically, I would never have thought about writing a book. Logic would have dictated that I give seminars on marketing or the challenges/struggles of entrepreneurism. Logic would have also told me that I would have a better chance to succeed in those efforts. (Logic can often be an excuse for not doing something while God is urging you to move forward.) Thoughts of doing these business activities just didn't click with me. The book idea was something that did click and caught me by surprise. For me, it became a dream that would not let go. I would not have even thought of such a dream if I had not allowed myself to consider many different opportunities, and if I had not asked God to stretch my vision of what those opportunities might be.

I decided to follow in the direction of my dream, believing that if God had given me this desire, He would help me find a way. I only had to step out and act on my dream. My part was to be faithful to what I believed God was leading me to do. I had to figuratively put my foot in the waters before they would part. I won't elaborate in detail about the journey my dream would take me on, but I can say to you again that as you dream your dreams, remember to pay close attention to the ideas that really resonate with you. Believe that God has plans for you and that things will work out. They did for me, even though there was to be a testing of my dream and faith. Certainly nothing happened overnight, but I have never regretted my decision. I would have had regret if I had not done anything about my dreams.

Finding God's Dream for You

Have you found what you could dream of doing with your life and talents? If you are not sure, look again at what motivated you in the meaningful life experiences you recorded in your journal or in this book.

As you study the list of dreams for your life, separate your stronger desires from your lesser desires. This is important because too many desires will clamor for attention and be confusing. Look for the dream that:

🍁 gives you a feeling of peace, *in spite of* logic or circumstances;

🍁 motivates you to want to do something right away;

🍁 seems to fit or fall into place—when you move away from that dream, you lose your motivation (Some psychologists would call this the "aha" syndrome—aha, I've got it!);

🍁 represents the seed idea or vision God has given you.

If God has a new dream for you, when you open the door that contains that plan, you will somehow "know." That knowing will give you a sense of peace about your dream even though much about it is uncertain. God has promised to guide you as you ask for that guidance: "In all your ways acknowledge him, and he will make your paths straight" (Prov. 3:6). This verse also reminds us that we need to include God in every aspect of our lives, even the little things, in order to receive direction from Him. With prayer and with God's leading, your dreams will not only be compatible with your life and talents, but also with His will and

His Word. As you surrender your plans, with trust, to Him, He will make them conform to His will.

Just wanting to know the will of God for your life implies you believe He desires to make that will known and then to guide you on the right path. Seeking God's will also implies that you believe He has your best interests in mind.

If a dream is ever contrary to God's Word, that certainly should raise a red flag in your mind. (When in doubt about a dream, consult the Bible for guidance.) God reveals His will in four different ways: first, through His Word; second, through our own judgment; third, through providential circumstances; fourth, through a clear inward impression of His Spirit on our minds. When these four indications agree, we can safely conclude that God is speaking. (For further reading about God's will, I highly recommend *The Christian's Secret of a Happy Life* by Hannah Whitall Smith.)

Put an asterisk by the dream on your list that most inspires you, even if it is something you have never done before. You should feel truly motivated to act on this dream. In the course of reading this book, you will be putting your dream, or heart's desire, to other tests of God's leading that particularly will help you determine if it is the right dream for you.

Deciding on a dream will help you start to answer the question of where you want to go and what you want to do with your life. Your plans may be marked by uncertainty, and if they are God's plans for you, they undoubtedly will require a walk of faith and testing. Still, I believe the hallmark of your dream is the inner peace we spoke of, even though that dream may not yet be clear. I happen to think peace within is one way God signals us to move ahead in spite of uncertainty. Not knowing how things will turn out is a necessary part of our journey and strengthening of our faith in God. (We begin to understand that as we learn to trust God for everything.)

Write your dream in your journal, and also here. *God has placed the following seed dream or desire in my heart:*

_____

_____

_____

_____

This dream, though still embryonic, may be overwhelming when you think about it. You may wonder, "Is my dream too big, or more than I can handle?" As you think about these questions, consider these thoughts. First, if your dream is from God, as I've stated, that dream *will* be bigger than you are. It is a myth to believe that if a dream is God-given, it will always be within your own capabilities and will be easy. The opposite is true. Why? Because the challenges of a dream help to build your dependency on God and your recognition that you can't do everything by yourself. When achievement comes because of your helplessness linked to the power of God, it will have a rightness to it. You will know that your ideas and abilities came from God, and that will bring a humility your own self efforts and success would not have brought. If you say, "I don't know if I can carry out my dream," you are right. But God working through you *can*.

Following our dreams, therefore, becomes a testing time, both for those dreams and for ourselves. Our dreams are being molded and shaped, and so are we.

Caroline—baroness, deputy speaker in the House of Lords, human rights worker, nurse

When I think of testing and God at work in someone who is following her dreams and heart, I think of Caroline. I first heard Caroline at a women's conference in California. She was one of the most dynamic and moving speakers I have ever heard. In her fifties, this native Londoner had the energy of someone in her twenties. This energy of hers and her own heart passions have motivated her throughout her life. She has led international fact-finding missions and lobbied officials from Bonn to Washington. She has worked with the Andrei Sakharov Foundation and Christian Solidarity International. Because of her unusual activities, Margaret Thatcher made her a baroness!

Wouldn't you think a baroness would lead a life of luxury and perhaps indulgence? Not in this case. In fact, Caroline dispels the myth that following your heart means seeking all the comforts life can offer. Caroline, in following her passions, often gives up life's most basic comforts and often risks her life to pursue her heart's choices of helping forgotten people. Baroness Caroline has taken to heart her father's advice: "It is important to put something back into the kitty of life." Here is her story.

"I try to do what's Christian. . . . I love working for those in Britain and abroad, helping students and as a nurse working on behalf of the ill, dying, and dependent people. In the international field I am trying to work for human rights, peace, and justice. I want to speak for forgotten people and take aid to forgotten lands. This is why I go to places like Armenia and southern Sudan.

"When I was a teenager I wanted to work in mission fields. I chose nursing as a first profession (rather than becoming a surgeon like my father). The special contribution of nursing is in the human relationship. It's that intimacy of being with people as they go through the journey of their suffering and maybe their death."

When receiving her training at London Hospital, Caroline was brought in contact with the poverty of the East End tenements, turning her into a moderate Labour supporter. Two years after she qualified as a nurse, she contracted tuberculosis and spent six months in a hospital. During her convalescence, she spent time studying for a sociology degree. Once she received that degree, she followed it with a degree in economics. She became a sociology lecturer at the Polytechnic of North London for nine years. Then she moved on to become director of the Nursing Education Research Unit at Chelsea College and also worked for the National Council for Educational Standards, trying to expose the decline in educational standards. In 1982 Caroline was created a life peeress, mainly for her educational campaigning.

Caroline now has an office in north London and works on numerous causes concerning human rights, health, and education. In the process of fostering international awareness, Caroline has helped raise funds for two hundred tons of vital medical supplies for Nagorno-Karabakh. She has returned to that country, a region of Azerbaijan (part of what used to be the Soviet Union) again and again. One time she had to walk for six hours through a snowy forest when bad weather kept her helicopter from landing. On another occasion rifle fire hit her helicopter and narrowly missed her head!

What does Caroline think of all this? She answered that question honestly when it was posed at

our breakfast table during a Women of Vision conference in California. Her answer reveals her humanness,
despite what seem to be super-human efforts and
accomplishments: "I go through a period of faithless,
fearful dread before each trip. I feel sick at heart and
think of all the things that could happen. I can only
pray that God's will be done."

In the Armenian capital of Yerevan, the parlia-
ment gave her a standing ovation when she addressed
them about conditions in Nagorno-Karabakh. Later the
head of the Armenian church, the Patriarch Catholicos,
told her: "Your help for our people has been beyond
price."

Caroline has done so much, but it is not it easy.
Her "dream-work" involves many challenges:

"My work often takes me away from home and
family. There is fear as I go into war zones. There is
also lack of pleasure and comfort. Armenia, for
example, has one hour of electricity a day. It is cold
and dark. At home, I can have a hot bath. This is
humbling to me. But when I am through [with such a
trip] I am inspired by the qualities of courage of the
people I have been with. When I am with people in
tragedy, I tell them, 'I won't forget you. I'll take your
grief in my heart.' I do, and it hurts.

"There are tremendous privileges in working
with people in dark and difficult days. They have
such dignity and are so gracious. I have made

friends and found new 'brothers and sisters' as I have left home and friends. Faith provides the motivation and the comfort. As Joshua 1:9 states: 'Be strong and courageous. Do not be terrified; do not be discouraged, for the LORD your God will be with you wherever you go.' And Matthew 25:40 reminds me, 'Whatever you did for one of the least of these brothers of mine, you did for me.' This calling is a privilege and a responsibility.

"God calls everyone to serve in different ways. Not all will go on cargo planes to war zones. I have enough health and energy to do it. But for everyone there is an opportunity. God won't ask you to do anything that you are incapable of doing. Turn your dream over to God. You can say, 'You have given me my life. What do you want me to do now? Take it from there with God. He takes us where we are. Our dreams can be His vision for us."

As I concluded my long-distance interview with Caroline, she was off again to Armenia and to Burma. It made me question what I was "off to," although I know not everyone, as Caroline said, serves in the same way. Some of us may not face danger and great deprivation as we pursue our heart and dreams. But we will have our own challenges, and we may have our own sacrifices to make. We will gain so much, however, that any loss pales by comparison. Having a dream and passion we believe in makes it all worthwhile.

Kim—writer, aspiring filmmaker/actress

Kim, a young woman in her early thirties, talks about her dreams and the challenges she faces, even though they don't involve risking her life as Caroline does. Kim started pursuing her dreams after a resource testing program revealed several choices for her life, one of which was acting. Kim had not found anything prior to that which she felt she could commit to wholeheartedly. Acting was something that struck a responsive chord with her. Kim talks about the challenges of following her dream, particularly within the entertainment industry.

"The first time I thought about a career in acting was when I was around twelve and watched 'Family' on television. I thought, 'I can do that!' It was a passing thought because I didn't have any direction or know that I could just decide to be an actor. Actors were just people you watch on TV or in the movies. Later, at age twenty, I decided to professionally pursue acting. I enrolled in drama school in New York, and my ultimate goal was to do feature films. Because that so far has not happened, I have asked myself what else can I do. I have qualifications, but I am lacking in connections. I think the next step in getting from where I am to where I want to go is to 'create my own break.' I have expanded into writing and would like to write and produce, making films along the line of Woody Allen or Spike Lee.

"Being a filmmaker is now my ultimate goal—I can do it forever and have some creative control. And I have written a screenplay which fortunately has been sold. That tells me something! I'm working on two other feature film projects, which I will try to produce and act in.

"Eighty percent of the time I have a belief I'm doing the right thing, that this is what I am supposed to be doing. Twenty percent of the time I wonder if it is worth it. There are bills to pay and sacrifices to make. Anything a person starts on his or her own has its challenges. I think when anyone is in the process of pursuing her dreams, however, there is no choice. The passion to be a filmmaker keeps me going. It helps me get up in the morning and makes me tick. Each day I have got to do something, even one thing, that will enable me to accomplish my goals. Anything I do I also put into God's hands first. I try to stay out of the results. This is very difficult to do. I have a need to be 'involved,' and it is a fine line to stay out of the results and yet walk toward your goal.

"It is frustrating seeing my dreams unfulfilled, but I do enjoy the process of having a dream. When I can concentrate on that, I get the most fulfillment and the best results. I wish at times I weren't so passionate about my dream. The rewards, though, are enormous. My career has helped me to grow and be focused on many levels, something I haven't done before.

"I think it is most important to share your dream where it can be nourished. Don't tell everyone. Many will say, 'You are crazy. Don't do it.' Start to share your dream only when you are strong enough. I believe we are all given different dreams for a reason, and it is important we follow through on them. But we won't know the reason at the beginning."

I like the fact that Kim emphasized the significance of three actions in particular: doing something she feels passionate about, doing something each day that moves her closer toward seeing her dream become a reality, and giving that dream over to God. This can be a delicate balance, but one that is *so* important.

June and Andrea—herb women

In a local paper I read about June and Andrea, women like Kim, who were thinking about what they wanted to do and what their choices could be. They eventually took an absorbing hobby and turned it into a business under the long, but unique, title Mad Mountain Women Herbals, Growers, Harvesters and Purveyors of Useful Plants and Their Prodigies.

June had spent eleven years in corporate America, running her own business in photography reproduction, while Andrea had worked as a hairdresser. June claimed that when the time came for a change, things started to fall into place. She commented: "I just decided that I wanted to live and earn some money at something enjoyable. First we had to find a niche to fill. Andrea had sheep as a hobby and an interest in herbs, so that kind of seemed like a logical place to start."[3] These interests led the women to the annual Sheep and Wool Festival held at a fairgrounds in New Hampshire, where they rented a booth to sell some of their herbal dyes. They ended up selling out most of what they had. Their new business was off to a good start.

Herbs filled the niche that the Mad Mountain Women were searching for when they pursued a business based on their hobbies and background. They don't measure their success, however, just by profits. June states: "My advice on going into something like this is to find something you enjoy and just stick your face right in it. As long as it's fun, I'd rather be poor and happy than rich and miserable."[4]

In hearing June and Andrea's story, as well as Kim's, I am reminded of how many women pursue ideas by first looking within themselves to find their own interests and strengths. One of the best strengths women display is tapping into and discovering their own assets and resources. It seems almost second nature to women. This, of course, is exactly what you are doing as you read through this book.

Diana—church worker, director of small group ministries

It is interesting as we hear from the women telling their stories to see how many different directions their heart's path leads them on. It's also interesting that several women were motivated by experiences they had in childhood. Diana would fit in that category. Some of what she experienced, or her feeling of lack from childhood, provided the fuel for her dreams. God used this to give her a new dream. She was able to turn that lack in her early life into goals and a work that ensures others do not miss out in ways she felt she did. Her heart motivations led her into an area of service in church work, first as a volunteer, and later . . . well, I'll let her tell her own story.

"I look back and for as long as I can remember, I can see God's hand on me. I had always assumed there was a God and went to church with my family. However, I never learned about Jesus except that He was a good man. I also had an innate understanding that I had to be good, to be perfect, in fact, and to earn my way in order for God to accept me into heaven. I recall one time feeling I had blown it at the age of six! My dad had punished me for lying even though I felt it was unjust, for I had not intended to lie nor did I think I had. It made a tremendous impression on me that I was now 'stained or marred'. . . no longer 'good' and my life would not be the same.

"My teenage years were often centered around the fear of death. I pictured myself dead and buried forever and ever and ever. In my longing to find some answers, I asked my parents if I could visit churches in the area by myself. I did and settled into a church in which the liturgy created a closer feeling to God—whoever He was. This continued into my college years. As a science major, I was significantly impressed with what I learned and saw in my course work and labs. It was reaffirmation to me that there had to be a creator. Life such as this could not just happen! Why would a God create such intricate life and beautiful matter and have it all die with no purpose? There had to be a reason for life as we know it!

"When I was accepted into a grueling medical technology internship, there was very little time for anything but my studies, lab work, and a little sleep. Sunday was the day to crash . . . no more church. There didn't seem to be any answers anyway. In fact, if there were a God, surely He would not be quite so hard to find. That's it, I decided, there is no God. Very quickly I began to feel very empty. I experienced the worst year of my life. I felt aimless and wondered why it mattered how I lived.

"A year later I settled in Boston, doing medical research. Maybe I would try the church routine again. I wished I could make sense of the Bible, as

I did with my other books. I prayed that if there were a God, perhaps He might help me find the right man to marry—someone who loved fun, had values, used good language, and stayed out of bars. Shortly thereafter I met Pete. He suggested I go with him to Park Street Church, and I found myself, at the age of twenty-three, being invited for the first time to a Bible study. I realized with my first visit that there was a message for me. I was beginning to hear some answers to the questions I had wrestled with for so long.

"Pete's friends were interesting and different. What was this 'Christian' business? Jesus wasn't just a good example? There is life after death? I don't have to earn my way to heaven? It was a gradual process of understanding for me, but a few months later at a Billy Graham Crusade I heard Billy say that God's Spirit opens our eyes to understand His truth. I heard answers that sounded as if God were speaking directly to me. Alone in my apartment that night, I quietly gave my life to Christ.

"Pete and I were married some time later, and we became involved as teachers in our church Sunday School. As a teacher in the Beginner Department, I kept one step ahead of the children as I learned more about the Bible! As we started our family and moved out of the city and to another church, I continued to volunteer with Sunday School, Pioneer Girls, Vacation Bible School, and music. Eventually it was apparent that God was calling me into ministry with women through the Community Bible Study. Being challenged to start a CBS study in my area proved a to be a test of my commitment. . . . It meant dropping off a tennis team! God honored my willingness and blessed our efforts with first sixty then two hundred women the following year; they came from many towns and churches in the area. The study continues to thrive today. It was through the excellent small group training and small group experience that God changed the direction of my life.

"Loving to study and a deep desire to discover more about the roots of the Christian faith, I began to pursue studies at Gordon-Conwell Theological Seminary. Spending many hours studying, preparing lectures for CBS, and developing leaders was an awesome privilege. I might add, however, I was at a point in my family's life where we all arrived home from 'school' at the same late afternoon hour. It was important to me that I not take time from my family to hide away with books.

"In June of 1994, I was offered a position back at Park Street Church as Director of Small Group Ministry. God had certainly prepared me for my first 'paid' position! I prayed hard over the model I would create for the growth of this ministry. This was a great time of trusting, and I said to God, 'If ever I need guidance, wisdom, and strength, it is now.'

Moving from a small church to a church of 2,400 people presented quite a challenge. I had previously said no to the position and certainly felt inadequate, but God in His faithfulness continually equipped and empowered me to do the best I could do. Pete also was very supportive, and when I started assisting at church services he commented, 'You look good in black!'

"Today I see how many of my classes in seminary helped me with the position as part of the ministerial staff of Park Street. I had been challenged by a professor that 'my head was in church history, but my heart was in evangelism and discipleship.' He was right and by switching my concentration, I was more aware of the challenges of a large city and a diverse church. Spending time helping to create small group communities of caring friends, committed to studying the Bible and applying it to their lives, as well as reaching out to others in the church and city, has been meaningful to me.

"I want people to know what is in God's Word, along with the power and empowerment. Why? Because I know how God changed my life! I was totally exhausted, thinking I could earn my way into heaven. The greatest gift I ever received was to know that through my identification with Christ, I could live with God eternally. To experience the new face of hope reflecting someone's understanding of this good news for the first time is a sufficient reward. There are many today in similar situations to my experience, and my motivation has been to help them find their way."

As I continued talking with Diana, I could sense the great satisfaction she has had with her heart's journey and with what she has been able to offer to others. She spent many years "working" in Christian ministry, until taking a staff position at Park Street. Diana is even now thinking of God's plan for her future. She is not a "settler" and wonders what is in store for her next. She is frustrated working mostly with those of faith and wants to reach out and use what she has learned, perhaps in a different setting. I believe Diana's restlessness is preparing her for her next adventure. I wish her well.

Your own dreams should be coming into sharper focus now as you've not only dared to dream, but gotten beyond placing limitations on what those dreams could be. As with Diana, you are trusting God's vision and leading for your life. It's important to continue to believe He has great plans for you, and never to doubt His love: "For I know the plans I have for you . . . plans to give you hope and a future" (Jer. 29:11).

It's time to consider the strategies and steps of faith that can move your dreams from the realm of wishful thinking into the reality of fulfillment.

Chapter Five

Making Your Dream a Reality

"When you wish upon a star, makes no difference who you are. Everything your heart desires will come to you." Jiminy Cricket sang this song in Walt Disney's *Pinocchio*. Wouldn't it be nice if fulfilling your dreams were as easy as wishing on a star? By now, you're beginning to see that it will take work to fulfill your dreams. You likely have an idea of what you would like to achieve and do, and now you can act on those dreams by asking the next question: "How can I get where I want to go?"

Beginning to specifically pursue your dream involves overcoming any challenges you might face and continuing to stay the course. You may have to weigh the possible risks against the possible rewards. All this will require you to manage yourself effectively and to continue believing that God is at work in you.

There is power in just beginning. I am reminded of one of my favorite quotations from Henry David Thoreau in *Walden:* "If one advances confidently in the direction of his dreams, and endeavors to live the life which he has imagined, he will meet with a success unexpected in common hours."[1]

Getting to Where You Want to Go: Setting Goals

As you advance in the direction of your dreams, it is important that you establish goals for yourself. Your dreams are possible, but the way to fulfill them is not always obvious. Goals can take you from simply wishing for things in your life to actively pursuing some of those things. Goal setting will also relieve some of the frustration that grows from feeling you are "sitting on the sidelines waiting for something to happen."

You have written down the dream you want to pursue. Now, can you write a goal, or working goal, that reflects your dream of what you want to accomplish? (A working goal is a goal that may be refined as you follow your work-in-progress dream.) For instance, if you dream of becoming an opera singer, starting a business, or working with children, list the goal or goals that could help move you toward that objective. In the first case, your goal might be to take additional musical training and talk to those who are already in the world of opera. If you wanted to start your own business, your goals might be to gather as much information about the product or service you plan to offer others and to talk to your potential competition. If you want to start working with children, one of your goals might be to learn more about volunteer opportunities at a local church or in the community.

You should be able to express your dream in a "dream-goal statement" that specifies what you want for your future. Record that goal in your dream-journal and also here.

My dream-goal is:

_____

_____

_____

_____

Goals are another way of stating what you want to achieve or become. They express your desires and what you intend to do about them. For instance, I know a businessman who has the desire to be the best speaker there is on his topic: how to sell and market digital printing. He has specific goals that he feels will enable him to fulfill his dream. Bill is working in many ways at making his dream come true. His dedication to his efforts is marked by excellence. It will not be chance, or luck, when he meets with success.

As you think about your goals, give yourself a reality check by asking these questions:

* Are my goals well-defined and specific?
* Are they based on my own heartfelt desires, temperament, and talents?
* Are my goals meaningful and exciting to me?
* Are they action-oriented, capable of being acted on?
* Do they seek to benefit others?
* Do I feel they help to forward God's purposes for my life?

Taking Action

If your goals meet the requirements just listed, you have every reason to believe they are realistic goals for you. Anthony Robbins, author and motivational speaker, suggests it is of utmost importance to act on your goals as soon as possible: "The most important rules that I ever adopted to help me in achieving my goals were those I learned from a very successful man who taught me to first write down the goal, and then never [to] leave the site of setting a goal without first taking some form of positive action toward its attainment." Robbins claims "ten days of small actions in the direction of your goals will begin to create a chain of habits that will ensure your long-term success."[2]

I would encourage you this day to write down not only your goals, but also the action steps that can help you to fulfill those goals. Even a small step or a "baby step" will help you create the momentum Anthony Robbins describes. I have found, too, that a dream is not nearly so intimidating if I approach it one step at a time. Taking everything on all at once tends to overwhelm most of us. If you can break goals and plans into smaller steps of achievement, they somehow seem so much more manageable. It also makes sense from a management standpoint to proceed carefully, letting things build on each other. Along the way you will gain knowledge, and most often one step leads automatically to the next step and the next.

Let's go back to the earlier example of becoming an opera singer. If you need musical training to fulfill this dream, your actions steps could be to find out where you could go for that training and to get names of recommended teachers. If you were thinking of starting a business, you could go to the library and look up books and articles that have to do with entrepreneurial opportunities, or you could look at the *Occupational Outlook Handbook* at your local library. (Librarians love to help and could assist you with your search.) If you wanted to work with children, your action steps could be to talk with leaders of civic and church youth groups and also parents. These conversations would help you find out what the groups have to offer children and what kind of volunteer help they need.

Before you continue reading this chapter, write down two action steps that you could take to further your own dream. These steps should not be too difficult to accomplish, but they should be focused enough to ensure that you are doing something specific about your plans.

Action steps:

1._____

2._____

Promise yourself that you will take these two steps within the next two weeks. This is crucial because you want to act while you are highly motivated and excited about your dream. The longer you wait to act, the more easily your dreams can fade and the more easily fear can begin to grip you.

You can review your action steps each week and ask yourself: *What information did I gain about my dream this week? What does this mean? Are my action steps carrying out and fulfilling the goals I have set for myself? Do I need to make any adjustments in my dreams or in my direction? What new action steps could I take?* It is important to give your dream flexibility to grow or to be redirected. Adjusting your dream doesn't mean you are abandoning it.

Whether you are thinking about starting a business, beginning a new project, doing something in the arts, etc., you too can ask yourself: *What is my dream for this enterprise? What would I like to see happen?*

Looking at where you are and where you want to be is an ongoing process. My husband, Len, along with his partner, Bill, the businessman of whom I spoke previously, always discuss each new idea that can build their business by answering two questions: "What is our dream for this business? What could we do to further our goals?" They next make a list of their goals and the action steps that are necessary to move them ahead. This becomes a way for growing their business and fulfilling their dreams for its future. You can approach whatever you are doing the same way, whether it is a business or not.

If you want to do volunteer or social work, you could take the action step of talking with churches or social service agencies to find out what help is being offered to people. Then you can look for the service that interests you. You might even decide to get a master's degree in social work. The more information you gather, the better you will know what is required of you and whether the opportunity appeals to you. This is true of almost any course of action you decide to follow.

You could be thinking right now that setting goals and action plans is not exciting because it involves thoughtful work. I realize that in our fast-paced "we-want-it-now" society, waiting for what we want can be frustrating. Our dreams seem so far off. Later we will talk about the stages of a dream and what to expect in following a dream. But for now I would like to emphasize that as you take action and move toward your dream, that action itself will start to energize you. You will be taking an active part in your dream's fulfillment, whether or not you see tangible results. Taking action has always made me feel movement in my own life. When I have a quiet period or a period of little activity, I am most apt to feel that not much is happening. (That is not always the case though, because there is an appropriate time to let things incubate.)

Remember Hannah Smith's words that God will go before you as you hear His leading and voice. That doesn't mean your path will be easy—it does mean you will go forward, stepping out in faith. In God's timing doors will open, and as Hannah stated, you won't have to bang them down. If you have to bang doors down, that is a sign that something about your dream is not in line with God's will for you.

If your first action plan doesn't work, try another and still another. Retune and refine as you go along. Persistence and commitment are the attributes that make for success and count for more than talent. I have known people who have achieved much yet are the first to acknowledge that others are more talented. They succeeded because they didn't give up. They also had definite goals and a plan, which they monitored on a regular basis.

A Part-Time Dream?

We have talked about preparing to follow your dream by asking, "Who am I?" We have talked about discovering your dream by asking, "Where do I want to go?" And we have talked about pursuing your dream by asking, "How do I get there?"

What else can help you get where you want to go? In addition to setting goals and taking action steps, you could pursue your dream as you have the ability and time. You don't have to do everything all at once. This means not only taking the small steps of gradually gathering information, direction, and knowledge, but perhaps following your dream "part time" between other activities. (Part time doesn't mean half hearted.) Remember Mary Ellen who combined part time work with her dream-activity of storytelling? There was also Michelle, who teaches three days a week, combining that job with motherhood.

I once met a woman, Patricia, who started out with a full-time job and used weekends, holidays, and spare time to pursue her dream. She had always wanted to be a professional make-up consultant in the entertainment industry in California. This came from a childhood dream and a childhood activity of "making up" her playmates and friends. Later in life she continued this activity, took needed training, and started getting clients. This all happened while she continued working her full-time job. Her dream business grew to the point where she could reduce her full-time job to a part-time job. She did two things part time: her beauty consulting and her office job. As her make-up business grew and grew, she eventually quit her part-time office job. Today Patricia is doing full time what she always loved to do.

I love the way Patricia followed her dream. She didn't throw everything to the wind early on, quitting a good paying job to go after that dream. She worked at her dream gradually and in "stages." I would like to add, too, that Patricia, like Mary Ellen, did not resent working at another job while she pursued her dream. She looked on her outside work as allowing her the opportunity to give birth to her dream. If you must work at outside jobs while trying to follow your dream, you can look on them as Patricia did—a way for you to entertain your dream while doing other things that provide economic stability.

You don't have to (and probably shouldn't) make major changes in your life in a hurry. I, for one, would never encourage anyone to just stop what he or she is doing to try something new. You should make major changes only when you have thought things through along the lines of the suggestions in this book and when events indicate the timing seems right (not perfect, but right).

Just as Patricia balanced two jobs, mothers of young children can follow their heart's path by weaving their activities around their roles of wife and mother (similar to Sherilyn in chapter one and Michelle in chapter three). I know a young mother with a baby at home and another child in first grade who loves to write and coordinate materials. She has looked for ways to write without letting it interfere with her family responsibilities. In visiting her child's school one day, she realized that it did not have a newsletter. Diane volunteered to write and assemble a newsletter that communicates administrative and class news to parents. Diane loves what she is accomplishing, both for herself and for her son's school. When her children are older, she may find other outlets for her writing. For now she is content to let her dream take the form of a volunteer, part-time activity.

Dreams and Conflict

I don't believe that a God-given dream, big or small, will conflict either with our talents or with where we are in our lives. God will not ask us to do something that we aren't equipped to do, nor will He give us a dream that does not harmonize with our lives. This does not mean, however, that God promises us a problem-free pursuit of our dream. Nor does it mean that others close to us will always support us in our dream quest.

I wish I could say that you will certainly get the support you need when you put yourself on the line and declare your intention to try new things. Unfortunately, this is not always true. Once I was speaking at a seminar, and during the break some women came up to me and expressed concern about their ability to find outlets for their heart's motivations and interests. Those around them were not supportive, for a variety of reasons. A couple of the women were almost in tears. I struggled to know how to answer them. I know that God has good things in store for all of us: "If you . . . know how to give good gifts to your children, how much more will your Father in heaven give good gifts to those who ask him!" (Matt. 7:11).

But I also know some people have a hard time understanding the use of talents by their loved ones. Some people like to control or they feel intimidated or threatened by change. It takes patience and wisdom to follow a dream in a way that neither alienates those in your household or world, nor causes you to sacrifice your dream and live a life of regret. Counselors, theologians, and doctors have all told us about the havoc we will undergo if we block out our innate abilities and desires. Our capacities clamor to be used. While using them brings us enjoyment, it also prompts us to grow. Unused skills or capacities can disappear or be diminished, thus diminishing the person. Be careful to respect and support the dreams and abilities of those you love, just as you expect them to do for you.

Your Personal Risk Quotient

As you continue getting where you want to go, you should also do a personal risk analysis. What do you stand to gain by pursuing your dream? What do you stand to lose? Writing a list with the pros and cons of pursuing your dream can provide you with fresh insights. I have a good friend who was weighing a decision about a major change in her life. She made such a list. When she looked at her completed list, she suddenly saw that all the pros of her decision had to do with her overall well-being—physically, mentally, and professionally. All the cons had to do with fear, negativity, or imagined outcomes. Suzanne said that organizing a written list presented her thoughts and options in a way that she could not have done in her mind. After working on her list, Suzanne's decision became obvious. She decided to follow her heart's choices and not her fear choices.

Now, take a few minutes and write your own list.

My own risk analysis:

Cons: What am I risking? (Be aware of real risks and "perceived" risks.)

_____

_____

_____

_____

_____

_____

Pros: What am I gaining?

_____

_____

_____

_____

_____

_____

_____

Do the things you stand to gain outweigh what you might lose or have to give up? Keep in mind that giving up is not always bad. It can mean giving up old habits and outdated patterns in one's life.

According to psychologist Abraham H. Maslow, writing in *Toward a Psychology of Being*, "We grow forward when the delights of growth and anxieties of safety are greater than the anxieties of growths and the delights of safety."[3]

We have talked about fear, and we will again, but it is wise never to make a decision that is based on fear. A fear-based decision could have kept author Jan Karon (see chapter one) from leaving her successful job in advertising, even though she no longer found it satisfying. Instead, she chose to leave that job and follow her heart and God's leading on a new path for her life. A decision to stay put would likely have been made out of fear of risking the unknown and not trusting God.

You too can make decisions based on what you know to be the best for you and not allow fear-driven decisions to keep you living in risk-avoidance and settling for "second best." Fear can compromise your dreams.

As you do a risk analysis, be aware that by balancing your dream and your resources, you are reducing your amount of risk. (This is what businesses do as they decide whether to take a risk.) Nothing is risk free, but building on the foundation of your own strengths and motivations certainly will help to offset your risk. And by now your dream should be a partner-venture with God as you trust Him for your future. That also reduces your risk factor.

Letting Go

Another important step in following your dream is to leave the results to God. Giving your dreams to God removes you from a position of control and allows for the unusual or even miraculous to happen as you adopt a "hands-off" attitude. None of us likes to relinquish control, but if we believe that God is working in us "what is pleasing to him" (Heb. 13:21), we CAN let go.

It is possible to hold onto dreams too tightly. Sometimes we learn the hard way that this approach doesn't work. I experienced this myself when waiting for my first book to be published. My dream started to consume me. I realized after doing my best, it was time to release that dream. Interestingly, it was when I finally did let go that a publisher offered me a contract. It took a while, however, for me to get to that point of release.

Part of letting go (as I have learned) is giving up whatever rigid attachment you might have to the final outcome of your plans. You can learn to enjoy every moment of your dream's journey even when you don't know what its outcome will be. As we learn to let go, God, with His infinite organizing abilities, can bring together the ideas, people, and circumstances when you need them. The more and more you experience this letting go, the more you will trust in Someone greater than yourself and accept uncertainty. You will still have goals, but you will be able to allow for infinite possibilities between point A and point B. This attitude will enable you to be sensitive to doors that might open or doors that might close.

Quakers used to call this kind of thinking "minding the checks." In other words, you will not be as likely to force solutions on problems, but you will be on the lookout for new opportunities instead. It is a misconception of society that we have to grab what is ours, with all the gusto we can. When things don't go our way, there is usually a reason. God's plan for each of us is much grander than what we could conceive of ourselves. And when things are right, opportunity will present itself. "Everything is possible for him who believes" (Mark 9:23).

Speaking of opportunity presenting itself, two women have stories of doors opening as they acted on their own goals. These women also followed their heart's path, and as they did so, whatever they needed was there when they needed it, sometimes in amazing ways.

Nadjia,—educator, television program producer, host

Nadjia has some fears about what she is doing, but she also has a lot of faith that everything will be okay.

Nadjia's father was an Arabian prince, an actor, and a speaker. Her mother was Swedish. She has inherited her father's dark good looks and his flair for acting and speaking. She has combined those talents with her heart's desires to find a need and fill it, in her case helping parents, children, and the community understand the needs of bringing up and educating young people. Nadjia seeks to be an advocate for these groups and to inspire them.

"I have been an educator for thirty years, mostly as a reading specialist. I've taught first grade through middle school and have also taught at the college level and at parent-teacher workshops. I've been trying to encourage other teachers in my workshops and bring them new resources and inspiration so they can go back and incorporate what they learn into their own classrooms.

"I have worked a lot with parents of troubled children and children who have trouble reading. That experience, and being in the classroom, helped me realize the need to communicate beyond the school. There is a tremendous need to communicate to those who are involved [with children]. Parents need to know what is going on (they often feel locked out), teachers often feel unappreciated, and children suffer from not having their needs fulfilled. Now I have become an advocate, and I have a chance to be a champion for these groups. For children, I want to be sure they get a quality education. For teachers, I want to make sure their dreams are not crushed, that too many expectations are not put on them, that they are not given tasks that are beyond them, and that they are appreciated (I've been there). For parents, I want them not to feel attacked for failing their children. Everyone values education, but all these groups are exhausted.

"My motivation is the need for children, parents, teachers, and taxpayers to be informed. It is a win-win situation if we all understand and can use knowledge that is helpful. This is what motivates me. Also, since I was thirteen, I have wanted to do God's will for my life. I also wanted to step out beyond the norm. I am a pioneer. I try to do three things: one is to help others, the second is to teach, and the third is to entertain.

"The last few years God has been slowly moving me from one place to another in my life. . . . I moved from head teacher of a state project to being back in the classroom. Then . . . in 1992 I took early retirement. . . . God opened other doors. I continued following my heart's desires and started producing school talk shows, with donated air time. Channel 36 PBS in Rhode Island opened their studios to me to do interviews. . . . I had my show, called *School Talk,* for several years. Originally production time with full studio staff and director were provided by Cable Vision Industries PBS 36 in Providence. At different times I had an office donated to me from a major business, due to a visionary person! Corporate sponsorship certainly was a big help.

"My new dream is to go from here to a broader viewership through PBS or commercial channels. I would like to have an expanded program that would include an audience and more video inserts and debates. There is a real financial challenge . . . but I do have contacts with WGBH in the East and with directors of major broadcasting companies.

"There is the fear of failure. How will I write a new show? It would be an embarrassment if I made a wrong decision. I am dealing with the waves of feelings that I have, and with capability and complacency. I have to hang on to hope and trust in God. There are benefits though, as I am learning more about God. With the strain of following a dream, there are benefits in seeing that dream

develop and mature in ways that I could not antici-
pate. When things look dark, faith, persistence, and
holding on to one's dream really pay off. I hold on
one day at a time."

As I reread Nadjia's story, I realize again that
she has been very sensitive to times that have required
a change in her life, and she has acted on those
changes. As she did, some wonderful things happened
that enabled her dreams to stay alive, confirming that
she had made the right decision. Pieces of her dream
came together, especially as she had office space made
available to her at corporations and studio space with
staff made available. Nadjia is very talented in presenting herself and her passions about education and people, and I am sure there are other doors that will open
for her in an equally timely way.

As Nadjia said, faith is important and so is holding on to a dream. Her story clearly demonstrates that
we don't always have to know all of the answers and
that provisions for our dream can come about in ways
we would never suspect. It's as if God and His rich uni-
verse conspire to help us along when we are on the
right path.

Claire—teacher, administrator, adventurer

Talking with Claire is to talk with someone who
is so alive that her enthusiasm and zest for life oozes
out of every pore. This is not because of some kind of

superficial, "I'm-happy-and-I-always-have-a-smile-on-my-face" attitude. It is because Claire is a can-do person and that attitude spreads to those around her. Claire has achieved the impossible, creating situations and possibilities that had never existed. She simply went ahead as though anything were possible. Talk about acting on one's dreams and goals in order to make one's dreams a reality! Claire's story shows what can be done when a woman's actions are fueled with passion and belief in what she is doing.

"I have been a teacher and administrator in public schools in special education. The main thrust of my work was the integration of the handicapped with the nonhandicapped, using music, drama, and dance. I have a God-given talent of playing musical instruments by ear and a love of children. Music is a common denominator that reaches everyone.

"I volunteered twenty-five years ago to use music as a vehicle for social and cognitive learning. I staged *Oliver* using retarded children and went on television presenting a documentary on what I was doing. I had no music degree or degree in special education. My superior in the Newton Public Schools secured a federal grant for me to continue my work. When certification became a big issue for teachers, the state of Massachusetts waved my certification. (I was already doing what they would certify.) I taught at Boston Conservatory for several years, both graduate and undergraduate classes, and then helped others to become certified teachers.

"Years ago I went with my husband on a business trip to China. My reason for going was to try to get into the schools. I met China's number one teacher (there actually is a number one teacher, so designated by the government) in their finest school. She had a hard time because she was teaching English and couldn't keep the children's attention. I said, 'I can help you by using music!' I taught English in this way in a hotel room for two weeks, and ended up with an invitation to come into China and teach.

"In 1979–1985 I set up the first public high school exchange between the People's Republic of China and the Newton Public Schools. For Americans, the exchange meant living in Chinese homes with host families for six months. In Newton, we had six children and two Chinese teachers. In Beijing, they had six students and two American teachers in a school of 1,300 students.

"I retired from the Newton schools in 1992 and from the Conservatory and had other dreams to consider. I began putting together a curriculum with five fourth grades, representing 110 children, in a school in Sudbury, Massachusetts. The principal asked if I would work on something with children in regard to a trip my husband and I were taking.

"We were going away for one year on our sailboat, from Bon Aire in the Netherland Antilles to the

San Blas Islands off the coast of Panama. We would be spending two months learning the culture of the Indians, a culture that is the same as the early 1900s. We planned to live on our boat. After two months we would go to the Galapagos Islands, and from there to the Marquises, French Polynesia, Tuo Motus, Tahiti, Figi, Tonga, and on to New Zealand. I would take a video of events and write a newsletter from every place we would stop. The trip was designed to help fourth graders understand cultural and human differences. I left them a big 'blow-up' map of our journey. It was very exciting.

"There would be times when we'd be at sea with no land in sight for as long as twenty to thirty days. And there would be risks, but that is life. People often are blocked by imposed control, either by others or self. When you sail, you pay attention to all the elements, and there is no control over them. You can't always control—so what can you do about it? Life is what you do with the shifting winds. It makes you who you are! You have choices. No matter what situation you are in, you have choices."

I am very moved by Claire's love of life, her love of children, and her willingness to do so much. She took action and constantly made her own opportunities. She did the best she could do without asking others permission for the go ahead. She just followed what she felt led to do, and is gifted to do, and that itself opened many doors of opportunity. The question we can ask ourselves is: "What can we give to others so wholeheartedly, and what doors will open as we do?" (Since the writing of this book, Claire has returned from her sea voyage, filled with glowing comments about its success.)

Is it really worth it to take those steps that move your own dream closer to reality? In the next chapter we will talk about some of the challenges that you, I, or any woman on a dream-quest might be facing. We'll also talk about the benefits of such a journey. I'm sure that all the women represented in this book would acknowledge both struggle and success as being part of their journey. Many would say that struggle has taught them even more than success.

Chapter Six

A Time of Testing

Your dream is about to be tested, and so are you. You have done a personal risk analysis and have made the decision to follow your heart's path, regardless of the risks involved. What's next? You can gain much by taking a closer look at the possible roadblocks or hurdles ahead. You should also take a closer look at the overall benefits of pursuing your dream (see chapter seven).

In seminars I have led, women had lively group discussion on the challenges they could encounter as they decided to follow their dreams. Such a discussion was extremely helpful because it showed them others will face some of the same challenges. They are not alone.

There is a sense of sharing and bonding, and strengthening of resolve. As you read this chapter, I hope that you will also know that you are not alone in the challenges you will face as you pursue your own dream.

Changing Your Attitude

What are some of the challenges you might encounter as you act on your dream-goals? I have already mentioned that you may have to give up control and be willing to live with uncertainty, realizing it is important to your dream's journey and outcome. We all want certainty and security, and when both are absent, we are apt to be restless or anxious. Following your dream might require you to make a paradigm shift in your thinking to welcome uncertainty and believe that solutions will emerge out of what appears to be chaos. Yet by adopting this kind of thinking, you can free yourself to experience life with all its adventure and mystery.

You may also have to adopt new ways of thinking about yourself, which could entail the definite challenge of getting rid of self-defeating attitudes. These could be anything from, "I don't think I want to attempt something new," to "How do I know I will succeed?" Those who speak about success tell us that if we are "results-oriented," we will most likely not tackle something new because we aren't sure of the outcome. This "I'll-do-something-if-I-can-be-guaranteed-it-will-work-out" attitude may keep you from achieving your dream. This is why it is so important to be grounded in the knowledge of your own abilities and be motivated by purposes that are strong enough to encourage you to take calculated risks. Also be careful that your attitudes don't limit God and what He can do in and through you.

As you seek to follow your dream, you may also need to increase your motivation to act on it. In other words, you may need to force yourself to get off your proverbial duff, and as Nike would say, "Just do it!" Inertia tends to breed more inertia, whereas being active gets us all on a roll. It is a lot easier to keep moving toward a goal when you maintain a constant forward motion in the direction of that goal.

Overcoming Circumstances

Your circumstances can be one of your biggest challenges. The challenge is to look beyond your present circumstances and not allow them to color your thinking or sense of reality. I remember many years ago reading the advice of Norman Vincent Peale—that we should always be "over" our problems, looking down on them, not caught up in them.

Having a vision of accomplishment always before you is one way to "get beyond" whatever your present circumstances might be. Don't be afraid to believe that you have a unique talent and a special way of expressing it. As mentioned earlier, this requires that you trust God. Such faith is a constant challenge, especially when things may look uncertain. Within the pages of this book, you've read stories of women who had to deal with just such a challenge.

I am also reminded of a story I first heard in childhood—the story of God choosing Moses to bring the Israelites out of Egypt. Moses seems so human when he makes many somewhat amusing excuses to God about why he can't do what God has called him to do. "What if they do not believe me or listen to me. . . . I have never been eloquent, neither in the past nor since. . . . I am slow of speech and tongue. . . . O LORD, please send someone else to do it" (Ex. 4:1-13).

Then there is the story of Gideon. When God told him, "Go in the strength you have and save Israel out of Midian's hand," Gideon replied, "How can I save Israel? My clan is the weakest in Manasseh, and I am the least in my family" (Judges 6:14-15).

Have you ever acted like Moses or Gideon, offering excuses to God for why you didn't feel you could carry out a task or a dream? The only way you will be able to overcome these feelings of inadequacy and any difficult circumstances is to trust God. Put simply, you must believe in your calling and in the One who has called you.

Finding a Mission

The primary challenge in pursuing a dream is staying connected with a purpose that continues to motivate you. Many today suggest writing a personal mission statement that can be used as a rudder to guide you through life. I know a college president who does this as his own personal and professional charter, and I know women who do this to help direct their lives. You have undoubtedly been thinking about your own mission while reading this book. Now you can begin to use that mission to set a course for your life.

Viktor Frankl, an Austrian psychologist and survivor of a Nazi death camp, claimed that we don't decide what our personal mission or vocation is so much as we "discover" it. He said:

> Everyone has his own specific vocation or mission in life; everyone must carry out a concrete assignment that demands fulfillment. Therein he cannot be replaced, nor can his life be repeated. Thus, everyone's task is unique as his specific opportunity to implement it.[1]

Jan—speaker, conference presenter, author, storyteller

Jan has an interesting story about finding her mission. If you were to meet her, you would immediately notice that she is a very animated person, talented in drama and speech. She is also obviously caring and loving. Jan often speaks to groups, including women's retreats. Her primary desire was always to have a home and family. As she has began to use her talents and discover her mission, however, she has found other dreams.

"Who I am today is affected primarily by three people: my dad, a minister; my mom, a communicator; and my husband, a pacesetter and encourager.

"Growing up in a Scandinavian family meant traditions and hard work. Family mattered. Growing up in a preacher's family meant moving a lot. This taught me to adapt, be hospitable, meet strangers, make friends fast. I see all of this as preparation for where God has brought me.

"My first ten years were lived in Illinois, then we moved south to Georgia. That was a major culture shock. I often wondered how my parents made that leap. The racial upheaval in the South in the fifties spilled over into my dad's church. He left the pastorate a disillusioned man and moved his family to North Carolina.

"When times grew hard financially, Mom went to work as a nurse. Dad traveled, selling church bonds and encouraging pastors. I was a latchkey kid, as the eldest, watching over my brothers and tending to household chores. I never felt impoverished. I thought this was how life was. Moms and dads worked hard, and kids did what they had to do to help.

"Growing up in rural communities in Illinois and Georgia, my dreams were simple. My parents provided my earliest dream model—love God and love your family. So I wished to be married, have children, and serve God. I see now how God fed and grew that simple desire in my heart. God became my teacher, instructing me through people, hard experiences, and events I couldn't orchestrate.

"After moving to North Carolina, my parents decided to send me away for my last two years of high school. I'd been in three different schools for my first two years, and they were worried about another change at such a crucial time in my life. Bob Jones Academy became my next home, and I surprised myself and everyone by thriving there. No rules and regulations hid the truth that this place loved music, drama, and literature. I was exposed to a wider world, even in such a narrow place.

"Following high school graduation I headed back to Illinois to Wheaton College where I met Jud, my future husband. My dreams were so small: get through and get married. I had never thought seriously about a career. Part of me thought, 'Why do I have to do something? Jud will take care of me.'

"My parents pushed me to study teaching. Professors encouraged my dormant gifts in writing and speaking. I listened and obeyed them all, like a good girl, struggling to know what I wanted. In the middle of the muddle, God remained that strong, silent presence.

"Like many, I graduated from college with more questions than answers. I returned to North Carolina, hoping for a wonderful job helping others. Meanwhile, Dad quietly read the newspaper, highlighting teaching jobs. I balked at all of them. 'I don't want to teach.'

"My dad smiled and calmly said, 'You'd be a wonderful teacher. You have the gift.'

"Finally, to quiet my parents, I agreed to go for an interview at the local junior high school. I reassured myself that no school would hire me since I'd never student taught. They hired me! Within two weeks, I knew my parents were right. I loved teaching. The following May, Jud and I were married. I taught while he attended seminary.

"Three years later we moved to Michigan where I continued to teach. After struggling with infertility, we received the exciting news that I was pregnant. Three years after Heather was born, our second child, Chad, arrived. My dream of marriage and family was complete. But God had more ahead for me than I dared to dream at that time.

"While living in East Lansing, we attended University Reformed Church. As part of becoming members of the church, we participated in a class which included discovering our spiritual gifts. Mine were teaching and encouragement. I was asked to lead the church's first women's retreat—and agreed with knees knocking. It was another unfolding of God's plan for my life and a glimpse into a dream I didn't know was mine.

"When I was thirty-six we moved east to Gordon College, where Jud became dean of the faculty. To come to Gordon was my husband's dream. He loved New England; I loved him.

"A couple years later, after our children were in school, I took a part-time job at the college working in campus activities. It was the beginning of a rich partnership with my husband. My husband knew the faculty perspective; I connected with the students. Later I became director of orientation, then assistant chaplain. Sometimes I spoke in chapel. This led to invitations from students to speak in their churches, opening up opportunities to speak nationally. I silently prayed, 'God, I could not have thought this up.'

"Almost nine years ago my husband became president of Gordon College. All my training in hospitality, meeting strangers, making friends, learning to adapt and flex prepared me for this newest stage. I love teaming up with Jud to tell and write the Gordon story. It's a fresh way to teach and encourage. It is my passion, my mission. I believe whatever motivates a person is his or her mission. Now my struggles are more with distinguishing the good from the best. It's about balance.

"Today I have a sense of harmony with what I do and how God made me. . . . I love being a wife and mom, but I also love using my gifts of writing, teaching, and encouraging. . . . To grow in love and knowledge of God is to learn to love and know yourself, since we are made in the image of God.

"To other women I would say, don't fear the silences. Some of my best growing times have been when I've been silent, lonely, and unsure of what the next step was, or if there would be a next step. Don't be afraid to trust God with all your heart's desires, wishes, and fears. I would never have dreamed my life would be such an adventure. I thought small sometimes, but trusted myself to a big God. Discover your gifts, your mission, what energizes you, and don't be limited or driven by outside forces. Enjoy the journey."

Jan found a real benefit in having a sense of mission, and you can see from her story that it evolved over her lifetime. She wasn't career oriented so to speak, and having a family meant everything to her. But you can see in Jan someone who throughout her life was tuned in to what her gifts were and sought to understand and use them better. She was also willing to ask questions about her life and was willing to wait on God for those answers. She is a good example of someone who didn't plan on doing certain things in life, but as she let her own heart's interests and mission lead, she found activities that continue to be immensely fulfilling.

I think Jan's story also illustrates that while some people are very goal oriented, and that is fine, others find their way gradually, just by following their heart and listening to God's leading. By the way, to hear Jan Carlberg tell one of her wonderful stories with her Norwegian accent is to be truly captivated and entertained. I could listen for hours. She has captured some of these engaging stories in her second book, *The Welcome Song.*

Attracting Financial Support

Some dream pursuits, such as starting a business, may require some financial help. I remember reading that if you have a money problem, you have an idea problem—get the idea right, and the money will follow. I think this means that if you are highly motivated, believe in what you are doing, and can document it in a good working plan, that plan can not only be used for outlining strategies but also for raising money.

People in the banking and business communities are willing to help if your goals and plans are clear. Over the years loan procedures have become more streamlined, and more lenders are willing to help women. Almost every state offers special assistance to women and minorities who are starting a small business venture. Often such funding programs offer one-on-one counseling. The Small Business Administration will help you find state and federal funding sources and also help you through the complicated application process. You should be able to find a Regional Small Business Development Center that can help you find and apply for a loan. Remember that when you are seeking grants, loans, and loan guarantees for a woman-owned business, you can also contact your state Office of Economic Development, located in the state capital.

If raising or obtaining money is important to your dream, complete documentation in a plan should include:

1. a statement of purpose,
2. a description of what you are doing,
3. marketing plans and market share projections,
4. a study of the competition,
5. financial requirements for working capital and capital expenditures,
6. a review of your background and the resources you bring to your efforts.

Belief in yourself and your dream-venture can count as much as documentation of that venture itself. Selling yourself and your ideas are both important. Remember too the women in this book who managed to overcome financial difficulty and follow their dreams.

Resolving to Persevere

When you think about what may be involved in pursuing your dreams, you need to sense the reality that what you are doing is not frivolous. You will need more than a slap on the back and a "You-can-do-it!" exhortation. In the quietness of your heart, you will need a steady resolve that you want to see your dreams come true, even though you have no assurance that they will.

It would be great if having a dream and seeing it come to fruition were a sure thing. Or would it? Such knowledge would take all the meaning out of what dreams are about: having a vision, stretching ourselves, growing our faith, trusting God, and doing the so-called impossible. Where would the sense of accomplishment be if what we were doing were a certainty? The reward of dream fulfillment wouldn't feel the same—it would be a hollow victory or success.

You may find the discovery of your dream comes during your greatest pain or personal challenges. By running from your pain or struggles, you could be running from your greatest dream. This is important to keep in mind when facing difficulties that could hold you back. God often uses a crisis in our lives to later accomplish good for us or for others.

Sue—artist

Sue is an example of a woman who faced her challenges head on and overcame them. Sue is an artist, a mother with grown children, now happily married, and living in the Southwest. She had a lot of pain in her past, and for many reasons, that pain was blocking her future. She was trying to create a new life, find a sense of direction, and experience the personal healing that would set her free. But she had been abused in her early years, and that abuse was still crippling her. Gradually, though, her pain gave way to dreams, and with those dreams her pain subsided. Listen to how Sue handled the hurdles in her life.

"My deepest desires regarding my creativity are to express myself in art and to express myself in words—to be heard. As I look back on the process, at times it seems to have taken forever! Enthusiasm came in spurts of productive highs, followed by periods of nonproductivity but with much visualization in mind.

"Near the age of thirty-six, I began looking within. I made major changes and took major risks. I broke the cycle of abuse I had experienced in my life by taking my children with me and leaving an abusive situation, never to go backward from that day on. I also connected with my psychological history, with what I brought with me. The desire to create was so deep in my soul, but I would put obstacles in front of myself. I realized that I created these blocks to expressing myself. When I began to understand one as an obstacle, it would go away. Then another one would surface for me to work through.

"I had to face many obstacles. First, I had to face the fact that I had never, ever gotten what I really wanted. (I think I realized for the first time that it was okay to want something, to ask for it, and to get it.) So the 'block' I put in front of me was to sub-consciously believe that if I ever got what I wanted, I would die because it would be so complete to me. I had an unconscious fear of death. One day I dis-covered the truth: receiving what I desired most in my heart would actually cause me to grow in way I could not even fathom. I left one fear behind.

"The second obstacle I faced was realizing that due to many deep disappointments as a child, I had an old pattern of thinking. If I wanted some-thing important, sometimes I would get it. But then it would be taken away. I learned to reject a good thing before I could lose it! This fear—of losing something good or having something good taken away from me—was very strong. Now, when I want something important but don't get it, I just let myself pursue another option, a backup plan.

"For years ideas crisscrossed in my head, but always without a plan, an actual strategy to begin. Never having a plan was a third obstacle for me. Part of my background included feeling shame when I asked for something I needed. If I received what I had asked for, humiliation and punishment always followed. Then I would not want what I had asked for anymore because it no longer seemed good. So to avoid shame, I never followed through with a concrete plan to accomplish what I desired most. I told myself I was never going to feel shame again. I made no plan. When I recognized this shame factor, my fear of planning lost its power over me.

"Another obstacle for me was that at times I found it hard to relate to someone else's agenda or schedule. It was not my agenda, my schedule, my plan. I finally saw the truth that I can learn from someone else's agenda and when I am ready, move into creating and following my own agenda.

"I was convinced that if I saw in physical evidence what I could do and I did it well, others would also see this. I had to perform well—another obstacle. Could I always do that? If I did not perform well, would I feel a failure? I began to understand the truth that even if I did not excel, I took a risk and did something! I was a better person for at least trying!

"For many years I said, 'I have to do this! I have to do this!' Believe it or not, those words were another way for me to block creativity and action. I spent most of my life telling myself those words of encouragement, yet those words were not what helped me to take my leap of faith! Now I say, 'JUST DO IT!'

"Since I have begun saying those words, 'just do it,' I am doing it! I am signing up for small art shows, completing the work for deadlines, entering a project in the state fair, making a big job change, and making definite plans for next year's large statewide art fair. I have never felt this way before. Now I am in the action mode . . . and it feels good!"

Sue had a lot to overcome—some self-imposed blocks and also circumstances that were part of her past. Although you might not have had some of the same struggles, you may recognize some of yourself in Sue's thought processes and fears. You may have to do what Sue did, gradually separate out erroneous or harmful thought patterns, replacing them with truth, healing, and a balanced perspective. Then, like Sue, you can move ahead, putting real or imagined obstacles behind.

You might write down any obstacles you feel are holding you back. Then address them head on, one by one, with a willingness to change and a desire to overcome each one. If this is just too difficult for you on your own, seek the help of a counselor or pastor.

Throughout this chapter we've looked at reasons why people give up on a dream, or feel overwhelmed by the challenge of pursuing a dream. Many of these reasons can be summed up in the word *fear*. Fear can so easily hold us in its grip. The best way we can conquer fear is to adopt a godly viewpoint about our pursuits. Remember that God always cares about our well-being. In fact, we are told to fan into flame the gift of God—our faith and the gifts we have been given. We are also told: "For God did not give us a spirit of timidity, but a spirit of power, of love and of self-discipline" (2 Tim. 1:7). When we trust God with our dream, we can walk right into the tunnel of fear and see light at the end of it.

Chapter Seven

Is It Worth It?

In the last chapter we looked at a number of challenges you could be confronted with as you act on your dreams and goals. Some of those challenges are daunting. In fact, you may be asking yourself now, "Why should I bother pursuing a dream when so much will be demanded of me? Is this dream more work than it might be worth?" Don't give up yet. You owe it to yourself to examine how you could *benefit* by following your dream.

When speaking to women's groups, I have encouraged them to ask, "Why bother? Why bother to leave my comfort zones, upset the status quo, or stick my neck out?" We then talk about what we think would make dream fulfillment worthwhile. Women all over the room comment about how they would feel as they start to achieve their dream. Just saying out loud what they would gain gives them renewed determination. Excitement builds. Everyone comes alive!

Experiencing Personal Growth

You have probably heard the saying that if you aren't setting goals and using the abilities you have, you risk not growing as a person (another form of risk). I once had a friend who gives self-management seminars say to me, "How few of us realize that we can grow, just as flowers or plants grow. We just have to nurture ourselves and make sure that we are doing things that can enhance that growth." Discovering a dream that motivates you and going after that dream will certainly help you grow as a person. That journey alone is rewarding in spite of difficulties you may encounter. Many of the women mentioned in this book would attest to this.

Actively Living Life and Trusting God

In talking with a number of women, I have been so moved to see that most have challenges, some great, some small, to conquer. For many, the challenges they faced inspired them to take some action. This certainly defies the myth that following a dream is just for those who have the time, luxury, or the money. If anything, too much comfort seems to be anesthetizing. Why work at something hard if life is already so good?

Remember Sue in the last chapter? She said, "I am in the action mode and it feels good!" There is little as satisfying as being in a place where things are happening in your life, and you are discovering purposeful living. It is exhilarating to see the future you desire start to unfold before you as you meet life's challenges head on and *live your life.*

As you search for those things that can bring purpose to your life, it will become more and more clear that you can't do things in your own strength and wisdom. This realization that you need help from God can help you learn more about God and about yourself. You will begin to develop a relationship of dependency and trust in God—something that you may have been missing.

Gayle—former CEO, now social activist

Gayle is someone who chose to act on her dream despite the challenges she faced. She left a high paying, high profile job because she believed there would be benefits in finding a new dream. She trusted God for those answers for her life and direction.

Gayle started out her career as a bridal consultant, eventually becoming a designer/buyer for department stores across the country. These were high-powered stores like Saks Fifth Avenue and Robinsons in California. She then switched to the production side, working for several manufacturers in Los Angeles. In

1972 she was approached by the Anne Klein Company, and in 1987 Gayle was asked to become president of Anne Klein II.

Gayle's rapid career advancements and good fortune were unusual. Even more unusual was that later she gave it all up. For Gayle, following her heart meant leaving what some people aspire to—success, recognition, and money. It was to lead her to a whole new area of commitment and to activities that provided a different kind of purpose in life. Here is her story.

"Everything I have done has been influenced by the experiences of my childhood, including my search for God. I was born into a home with alcoholic parents. We lived on the best street in the biggest house, and my father was an important man in town. At age four, I decided to shield what was happening in our home from the world and also from my brother, who was one year old. These two decisions set the course for my life. As a child, I also confronted my parents because I was fully aware of what was going on. In making these decisions I developed a very high sense of responsibility for family. Secondly, in confronting my parents and paying the consequences for that, I learned to stand up for what is right. That prepared me for later in life.

"The situation in my home—my mother was physically abusive—spurred my search for God. I knew there had to be something better than this.

Home was a nightmare.

"My foundation was laid early and would influence the rest of my life, especially having a strong sense of responsibility and boldness to confront wrong action. During those years, however, I repressed a lot of anger. I did what I had to do, but I had no outlet for my anger. This took a toll physically, and I had to have some operations. Later in life I learned that I needed emotional healing to experience the power of forgiveness. The night my mother died God provided a miraculous healing as we both asked each other for forgiveness. (I never needed any more operations after that!)

"I think the real lesson of my life is that God never lets us lose anything He has allowed us to experience. All my hard life lessons and tough experiences He used for my benefit.

"After college I wasn't prepared for the career I got into, but I relied on my high level of responsibility to become a better executive. . . . I was with Anne Klein for almost twenty years. I worked on the West Coast, tracking their distribution, because it was becoming a big market. . . .

"I began working, observing, and promoting the line in the stores. Because of that personal attention, the business grew rapidly. Anne Klein made me vice president of marketing, and I was spending half my time in LA and half in New York. When I was asked to take over the presidency of

Anne Klein II, my foundation of accountability and
responsibility helped me. It made me more successful in the business world much sooner than I
had expected.

"I retired from Anne Klein at the end of 1991
and came back to LA to volunteer my time in the
field of education. I began to work with a few different groups in low income area schools to help install
character education programs. I now work with an
organization that has a curriculum enabling parents
to help their children succeed in school. We'd like to
set up parent centers so they can work in partnership with principals and teachers. We're also hoping
to pull some corporations into the program.

"I left Anne Klein II to work for God. I wanted
to do what the Lord wanted me to do. . . . Selling
another ten million garments suddenly seemed less
important for me.

"My advice to others would be first to know the
Lord and follow His leading in your life. Obviously,
pursuing your heart's desire takes courage, and yet
if you take those steps of faith and act in courage,
God honors that. It is exciting, but you will be
stretched and you will grow. God points the way and
provides!"

Gayle left a prestigious job for social and community work that would meet her heart's needs and
the needs of others. Her story dispels the misconcep-

tion that to follow a dream is to seek fame or fortune. In her case she left a certain amount of both to be involved in activities that had more meaning for her that honored God in a special way.

Looking Back with No Regrets

In addition to experiencing personal growth, actively living life, and trusting God, another benefit of pursuing your dream is that you will be able to look back on your life with no regrets. It is hard to put a price tag on the great personal satisfaction this will give you. It has been said that to have a dream but never pursue it is to kill one's spirit. To live a dream is to find JOY.

A young pop singer, Cathy Cornell, talked of the price she started to pay because she had given up on the things she loved and replaced them with things that didn't motivate her. She had gotten burned by a record producer and decided to quit singing. She took a manager's job at Federal Express, but that didn't last long. She explained, "I discovered that when you give up your dream, when you do something else, it's going to take its toll somewhere. I gained weight; I got depressed."

Now Cathy is happy that she has gone back to being a singer and offers others this advice: "If there's one thing I want to get through to people, it's 'Go for it—for your dream.' You'll be your happiest if you're doing what you do best."[1]

Elizabeth Kubler Ross, a prominent psychologist/counselor/author who has researched death and dying, said that on their death bed those who protested dying the most were those who suddenly realized they had never really lived. They literally screamed their protest! This is a chilling and sobering thought. How sad it is that some people die with the music still in them.

Life expectancy has been going up over the last three decades. Thus, we have an even greater opportunity to live fruitful lives. Many people quit working between ages sixty to sixty-five and are still in good health. This means that the average person will have another twenty years or more of life yet to fill. More and more older people are "doing" something in their post-retirement years. I loved a headline in the *Boston Globe*: "Growing Number of Elderly off Their Rocker and Loving It."[2]

The article opened with the story of Shana, who at age seventy attained her dream of getting her pilot's license. Then there was the story of Dorothea, a former nursing home administrator, who graduated from Northeastern Law School at sixty-four and passed the bar at sixty-five. She became a lawyer. Marilyn, another senior mentioned in the story, is sixty-three and a retired graphic artist who now travels to the Andes to help design and market native sweaters. These older women can help motivate all of us to follow our dreams, even in our older years. Don't live a life of regret.

Margaret—speaker, storyteller, author

Margaret is an older woman, like those in the *Boston Globe* story, who certainly has followed her dream. She has no reason for regret. Margaret is eighty-something and probably has twice the energy and enthusiasm of many half her age. When you add a generous dose of humor to that mix, you have a fascinating woman. She also has incredible faith. As Margaret puts it, "I love to tell the story of Jesus and His love for us, and I feel I can do it in a way that is not preachy." Margaret tells that story often. In fact, it has become a focal point of her life/work. She leads quite an active life, traveling around the country speaking to women's groups. What inspires her to give so much of herself? I'll let her explain.

"I was six years old when I decided I wanted to give my heart to Jesus, and I walked a long church aisle to make that decision. At six years old I felt I knew the answers to the questions that people are still asking: *Who am I? Where did I come from? Why am I here? Where am I going?* I knew I belonged to the family of God, and that God had a purpose and plan for my life. I knew ultimately where I was going. Philosophers continue to discuss this. But when you come to know Jesus, you have the answers at any age, even age six! There is a simplicity to the Gospel, and it takes a childlike faith to understand it.

"I have never lost my faith. My father, who was a minister, always stressed, 'Don't lose the wonder of salvation.' My father also taught me to love words and to paint pictures with words. When I was young I made up all kinds of stories, and I told everything like it was gospel. Not a bit of it was true! I told stories and fantasies like you wouldn't believe.

"From the time I was two I wanted to be a nurse. I seem to have this romantic and practical side to me. Later I did become a nurse, and it made me disciplined and organized. I did all kinds of nursing. What I loved most was private duty—I entertained with stories! Some of my patients begged me to stop because they laughed until it made them hurt. They also pleaded with me to write down my stories.

"After finishing nurses training, I married a man who was a minister and worked until our children were born. I stayed home when the children were small. As they got older, I went back to nursing part time and then full time. Eventually, I became a college infirmary nurse, which was right before I started writing.

"In my late fifties and sixties I started writing short stories. But I think back to when I was in my thirties, and I wrote stories even then. A man doing workshops for Sunday School teachers did a seminar for our church. He stayed in our home. I was quite busy because I had three of my own kids, two more kids staying with us, a house to take care of, and church duties to prepare for. So I told this man, 'I just have homemade soup for dinner. And you can do anything you want to do, but I have to clean up after dinner.'

"When we finished dinner this man said, 'What can I do?' He had five kids himself, so he understood.

"I said, 'You can tell my kids a story while I tidy up.'

"On Sunday our guest was with us all day. He said to me, 'I've got to write a story for the *Baptist Standard,* and I am not looking forward to it.'

"I had laundry to do, so I said to him, 'You wash my clothes, and I will write your story!' I did write his story, and he sent it to the *Standard.* The editors later commented that it was the best story they ever received from him. As a result, I ended up writing a story every month after that for the *Standard*, under my own name.

"When my mother died in 1977, I realized my stories would die. I wanted to write little stories to keep. I decided to start writing in order to have stories for my children. I brought my stories to a writer's conference at Gordon College in 1982 and was encouraged. In 1983 I wrote my first book, *First We Have Coffee.* I also started traveling. My first trip was to Tacoma, Washington, to speak to one thousand women. I had never spoken except in church.

The woman in charge of the retreat asked me what I wanted for an honorarium, and I didn't know what an honorarium was. I said, 'Just give me what you gave the last speaker.' Then I found out the last speaker was Shirley Boone! I have gone back there every year.

"I use a lot of humor when speaking. The joy of the Lord is my strength. Joy is of the spirit. My greatest motivation is this: I love to tell the story of Jesus and His love. I love travel, love people, and love my message because I've got something to say. You only have something to say when you get the message from God.

"In the past I used to entertain, but now every story has to have a message. I memorize everything. My mother always said, 'It is very simple to serve the Lord. You just do it. It is simple, but not easy.' She also said, 'Use whatever is in your hand; whatever skill you have, use it.' Mother cleaned houses and said, 'Are you willing to pick up a scrub brush, or whatever you have in your hand to do, and do it?'

"My husband, Harold, died in 1991, and before he died he wept when he realized the unusual gift God has given me to tell of His love through stories in a nonthreatening way and still get my point across.

"I still say to others, 'Live in the present. God will guide you.' A favorite verse I have on a plaque expresses how I feel:

> *Even when I am old and gray,*
> *do not forsake me, O God,*
> *till I declare your power to the next generation,*
> *your might to all who are to come (Ps. 71:18).*

"I tell my grandchildren, 'You are my reason for living.' And I love young people. I have always felt blessed and privileged, and I have been in some hard places. I know I can trust and obey God, one step at a time. Victory is putting one foot in front of the other. Women in their eighties have just as much power, and that power can be a ministry of prayer, even if in bed.

Hearing Margaret Jensen talk is to listen to a woman with unique gifts and talents that have been evidenced throughout her lifetime. In her later years, and in God's timing, she has found herself speaking and writing on a regular basis, at the age when many would be ready to retire. It is wonderful that she continues to use those talents in ways that bring so much blessing and joy to others. Margaret is known for her best sellers, *First We Have Coffee,* and *Papa's Place.*

Margaret is the mother of Jan, whose story was in chapter six. The two of them are a team, not only as mother and daughter, but in their speaking and storytelling. You could call them "The Dynamic Duo." They have started sharing many of their speaking engagements as they travel across the country with their presentations. I asked Jan how she felt about that. She said, "This is one of the greatest gifts, because I moved away from home after I was sixteen. It truly is a surprise gift from God that He could arrange for Mom and me to meet all over the country and do things together. This happened after my dad died. It is a privilege to have a co-ministry. We enjoy each other's company, and we can learn from each other now. We witness a tremendous response when others see the two generations working side by side. It is one thing to pass things down, but another when together we tell our story. We recognize this and pray for our children. It will be their choice whether the branch goes on to another generation."

I have to add that I heard Margaret speak in chapel at Gordon College and say to her audience, "And when I am on the road speaking . . . ." How exciting to hear those words come from an eighty-four-year-old woman! Talk about redefining old age.

Minerva—artist

Minerva is another woman in her eighties who is actively pursuing those things close to her heart and living a full life. Before meeting Minerva for an interview, I spoke with her on the phone. (I knew she was an artist and someone who never let any moss grow under her feet!) I asked her, "What are you doing now?" Her answer was that she had three children's books almost ready to send off to publishers, books that she had illustrated herself. I asked her when she was going to put her feet up, and she said, "NEVER!" What an inspiration it was talking with Minerva. Later we met, and she talked about her life and the dreams she still has.

"I had a grandfather who came to the U.S. from Germany. He was a woodcarver from Bavaria. He had carved a bed with angels as the four posts and their wings holding the canopy. He entered this in the World's Fair in Chicago in 1893 and won first prize. The bed was sold to an Italian princess. My grandfather used to sit me on his lap and teach me how to draw simple things like birds and flowers. At age eleven, a cousin in this country bought me a watercolor set, and I was off and running.

"Whenever I saw the word *art* it was like music to my ears. It did something to me. I did so much art in high school that my teacher said, 'You should be going to art school.' I ended up dropping out of school after two years because it was hard, although I did well in art.

"When I was sixteen years old I had a chance to paint portraits of three famous aviators, Captain Koehl, a German baron, and an Irish aviator. They had flown from Europe to America in the first westward flight. Captain Koehl was coming to my hometown. He was to be given a parade. I wanted to paint his picture and give it to him, and I also painted the other aviators. At that point I hadn't yet gone to art school. I did the painting and had it framed, and I was the only female allowed to be on the platform that day. As I gave the painting to Captain Koehl, he bowed low and kissed my hand. I was so happy.

"I really wanted to go to art school, and my mother decided I could go. I went to the Cooper Union School in New York, a completely endowed school for young ladies with artistic talent. (The school is still in New York and has expanded its program.) Six hundred girls applied, and ninety were accepted, including me. I had dreams of becoming an artist, but I never thought it would be possible. I had an inferiority complex when I was growing up, and didn't come out of my shell until I was twenty-two. But I also had a deep faith and a good upbringing.

"Being an artist was always my only goal. I was always dabbling in art and pursuing it in my own way. That is what I loved. I also loved Greek mythology, maybe because my name was Minerva, the Greek goddess of wisdom and art!

"I majored in magazine illustration at Cooper Union. I was in seventh heaven. Here I was in a school with some of the best instructors. One of my teachers had paintings in the Louvre in Paris. I went to art school for four years. I was going to set the world on fire when I got out and do magazine illustration. In a class of thirty, I ranked third highest. (I had also taken sculpture, design, and oil painting.)

"When I got out, I didn't know how to pursue a job. One thing I did at age twenty-one was paint twenty-three murals for Victor's Restaurant in New York. Shortly after that I got married and had two children, both girls. I continued with my art work, selling it by mail. I was also selling little miscellaneous things to local businesses and did newspaper commercial layout. I did wallpaper designs for Schumacher and Waverly. Unfortunately, I ended up getting a divorce.

"Eventually, I sold some of my designs to a company in New Hampshire for a party line they had. They asked me to come see them and design a line for Woolworth's. I went, but I also think they wanted to see how I would fit in with the seven men in the art department. I had been living on Long Island, was a member of the Nassau Art League of Long Island, and had won awards for my paintings. I moved to New Hampshire and took over designing the line we had talked about. I became the art director and set up trade shows across the country for the company.

"Before I left for New Hampshire, I had never expected to leave my home. But I had a dream and felt that God was showing me it was okay to move. I would be happy. In New Hampshire I started the Nashua Art League because I wanted to do more with my life than just work.

"I soon met a Christian man named John, who was to become my second husband. . . . I continued to paint and do watercolors for my own gratification. This was probably the happiest part of my life. John and I were married for thirty-nine years before he died. We had a great life together.

"Later in life I did some other things as a freelance designer for various firms. I still haven't accomplished some things I would like to, such as my dream of being an illustrator. Now in my eighties, however, I am illustrating books and writing my own stories to illustrate, which is where I started out at age twenty-one. In some ways I have been sidetracked too many years. Lord willing, I will keep illustrating books and reach my goal and dream of being an illustrator. Now I have to sell a book to make it come true.

"I don't feel that I am old. I feel that I am just starting out on a new venture. I have a lot yet to do in this world. . . . I don't think because people have reached a certain age that is the end of things. If they are in good health, they can look for more opportunities, and they can take whatever talents they have and use them. They can keep doing what they enjoyed when they were younger. Older people shouldn't put themselves on the shelf and let the world go by.

"I would say to older women that if you continue to do things, it will help you feel young. I am always planning, even simple things such as raising tomatoes, cooking, having people over, and taking trips.

"The desire to be the best in what I do keeps on motivating me. I must better myself, and that is always a challenge. But self-gratification and applause are the benefits. My advice is 'Go for it!'"

I am so impressed that Minerva keeps pursuing her interests. She doesn't use the "I'm too old" excuse. Minerva and Margaret are both good reminders that older women can still have dreams and continue to stretch themselves. Dreams are not just for the young but also for the "young at heart." We have all heard of people who, as they age, give up on life and their lives literally come to an end, sometimes prematurely. It seems when any type of dreams die, spirits do, too, and often the body as well.

Commitment that Develops Character

Another benefit of being committed to your dreams is that your character will develop as you dedicate yourself to your efforts. You have to be willing to pay the price and to endure and achieve your own form of greatness. Minerva is following dreams that she had at twenty-one. She never gives up. I often think of young professional ice skaters, such as Paul Wylie and Nancy Kerrigan. Their untold hours on the ice over the years have helped them achieve their dreams. Every time I see ice skaters, and the results of their amazing dedication, I am motivated to have that kind of commitment. How many hours at the "rink" might you and I have to spend to excel in whatever we are doing?

Following the path that your heart's desires are leading you down will force you to make conscious decisions. As you look at these choices, you can ask yourself, "What are the consequences? Will this choice bring happiness and help to others?" Heart choices will always be positive. You are not the only one who will benefit from them.

Don't we all wish that our dreams would come into being overnight? Of course, that doesn't usually happen. In the next chapter we will look at the natural sequences of a dream unfolding. This will help you gain a better understanding of where you are on your dream fulfillment quest. You may be farther along on that quest than you thought!

Chapter Eight

Understanding Your Dream's Journey and Your Part in It

By now you have carefully thought about your dream, and that dream has no doubt started to grow and become more focused. Meanwhile, you have probably found that along with the activity and busyness of pursuing your dream, you encounter times of inactivity or waiting. Those times can be especially confusing, hard to interpret, or even discouraging.

Realizing, as has been stressed, that this waiting period is necessary and doesn't mean your dream is forgotten, will significantly help you look at your journey with new insights and patience. You will see that God isn't just at work when things are going well. To really believe that would be to miss seeing God at work in the troublesome times. In fact, the awareness of God's partnership with you in your dream may become the most obvious during dark and lonely times.

Your dream (or dreams) will require a period of cultivation before it is fulfilled. All dreams must go through a refining stage. This will strengthen your faith and trust in God. Becoming aware of the stages of pursuing a dream can help you chart your progress. You will then be able to look at any given moment and better appreciate the whole of your dream-journey.

There are four distinct phases of a dream. In the first stage your dream is unclear; in the second stage your dream is tested, suppressed, and almost forgotten; in the third stage you are helping others and seeing their dreams fulfilled, with your own yet unfulfilled; in the fourth, your dream reaches maturity and fulfillment. These stages, or phases, can overlap, but they represent the growth process of a dream.

Most of us would love to go quickly from stage one to stage four, denying that stages two and three are a normal part of moving our dream toward reality. But each stage helps to grow our dream *and* to prepare us for that dream. We can take our cue from nature and the planting of a seed. We plant the seed (our dream), wait for it to blossom, think about digging it up to see if it is still there (but shouldn't), and water and tend to other plants in the meantime. (We continue to pray that God will water our dream in accordance with His will and timing.) Then, someday, perhaps when we least expect it, our dream comes into full bloom. It is time for celebration!

Dream Stage One—An Idea!

Let's talk about the first stage of your dream. This stage is the period when an idea or seed thought begins to grow within your heart and mind. You are unsure of its full meaning or scope. You only know that something has caught your interest and imagination in a way that has never happened before.

I can assume at this point that you have had such ideas, and they have been developed further in the reading of this book. I sincerely hope you haven't underestimated the significance of those early embryonic dreams that have taken up lodging in your heart. I've stated that stage one, or the early stages of dreaming, is when most dreams can die. In fact, they do very often die at this stage because the dreamer does not recognize their value or potential or lacks faith in her own ideas or in God. Sometimes, too, dreams die at this stage because of others' discouraging words.

As I think of this early stage of a dream—when it first takes hold—I am reminded of an amazing story about a woman who lived over one hundred years ago. The fact that she lived so long ago is what makes her story all the more unusual. Bina was a school teacher and a single woman who lived in the Midwest, traveling by horse and carriage. Bina observed some of the injustices of her day, and with that observation came a growing restlessness to do something about them. She witnessed children whose mothers had died and were then sent away to orphanages, even though their fathers were still living. She wondered, among other things, how women and the needs of their families could be better provided for. Many families were struggling just for existence. But what was an unmarried teacher to do? Something, however, was happening to Bina. She not only saw real physical needs going unmet, she saw those needs with the eyes of her heart. As she reflected and was moved by her observations, a desire started to grow within her. She wanted to do something to help, but what was that something to be?

Bina had to take action—she could no longer remain silent in the face of such troubling circumstances. (Restlessness, as we've discussed, can be a signal of a shift in one's life.) She wanted to be a catalyst for change. Suddenly an idea crystallized. Why not find a way to help women and their loved ones handle the adversities and circumstances of life? Bina made a decision. She would approach insurance companies and ask them to consider providing insurance for women, a dramatic idea at the time because insurance companies only covered men. But wherever she went, Bina only seemed to get doors slammed in her face. Many probably considered her revolutionary. She knew she didn't have the money to follow through with her idea, so she approached others with a request for financial support. She had the extraordinary vision to believe that a fraternal benefit system could be of great help to women and their families. It was so important to her that she decided to turn that idea into her life's work.

Bina's dream kept growing, and she refused take no for an answer. She was finally able to secure a five-hundred-dollar loan from someone, and she was off and running. I call that the "foot in the door." Now the door could no longer slam shut on Bina's dream. At the age of twenty-five, with a relatively small amount of money and a great deal of conviction and courage, she was able to start her own company. That company exists today as Women's Life Insurance Society in Port Huron, Michigan. It has grown to be a very substantial and viable company, and to my knowledge, it is the only insurance company that was started by a woman, is managed predominantly by women, and focuses on the needs of women and their families.

I visited Bina's company some time ago. It is housed in a beautiful historic building and stands as a testimony to one woman's dream. I entered the building and immediately saw descending staircases, flanking both sides of a center landing, with steps leading down to the lobby. I walked up to the landing and looked at a large picture of Bina hanging on the wall, as if she were overseeing all who entered. I stood in respect for a woman who would be so proud if she could see the fruit of her early dreams.

Bina's story shows how circumstances, awareness, and desire all conspired until a dream was born in her heart. That dream was unclear at first, and I'm sure it went through the many phases of a dream, although reading her story makes it seem everything happened at once. It obviously didn't.

Dream Stage Two—Put to the Test

Perhaps, like Bina, your dream has started to take hold. Maybe you've observed needs and also possible ways to meet those needs. Your dream may be about to enter the *second phase*, the testing phase. If you are a dreamer, remember that God will have a test for you. It will involve the stripping away of your dream to reach its true value. This is really a refining process more than a test; God is developing your character to match your dream. Such a stripping removes any false or selfish motives. Undoubtedly, you will need to get rid of some things before you gain what you are seeking. This is true for each of us.

If you feel you are in stage two and wonder whether your dream will ever come together, remember your responsibility in this stage is to step out in faith, pursuing what is in your heart. The pieces of your dream will come together in their own time and way. Bina's dream was tested. She was no doubt at the end of her rope when someone assisted her in keeping her dream alive. It may be the same way with you.

Just when you think all is lost, a door may open. During this testing phase it is easy to feel that your dream will never be "real"—you may feel you are walking through a valley that seems dry and parched.

During my first experience at writing, when my plans were being tested, I would ask questions such as, "Does this make sense? Do I feel at peace about my dream even though it is bigger than I am? Do others relate to my topic?" These questions became a barometer of my progress. When the answers to these questions were affirmative, my passion to communicate what was in my heart only became stronger.

Understanding that your dream will be tested—to improve and direct it—will help you view this phase as beneficial and not hurtful. Just that viewpoint alone could make the difference in your perseverance. You may also need to ask God whether you need to do any redefining of your dream. And be open to that leading. God may use others or your own convictions to nudge you in this direction. Every once in a while it doesn't hurt to stop and take a reading of where you are and ask what it means. This can act as a purification of your dream. It is also good to view pursuing your dream as an *ongoing* journey. Like any journey it will have detours and delays, and you might feel lost for a while. But your destination is in mind.

Here are some additional questions you could ask yourself in the testing stage of your dream.

- Does my dream make me a more authentic person because it draws on my God-given talents and temperament?
- Do I feel at peace about my dream in spite of the challenges I am facing?
- Do I feel passionate about my dream—does it still motivate me?
- Does my dream benefit others, without harming anyone?
- Do I need to make any changes in my dream?
- Have I continued to pray for God's guidance?

It can be a source of frustration to know that you may be passing the tests and doing the right things, and STILL not experiencing fulfillment of your dream. Take heart! The waiting/testing period is but a precursor to stage three—the time when you will be actively involved in helping others while waiting for your own dream to reach maturity. All this will prepare you for stage four—the eventual blossoming of your dreams and plans.

Joseph's Strange Journey

The story of Joseph is not only a great story but also an inspiring lesson in the unfolding of God's plan—with its timing, purpose, and fulfillment of that purpose. Listen to the familiar story again. You may have missed seeing the different stages of God's dream for Joseph and the principles involved in each stage. Joseph's story is about trusting God in whatever circumstances you may be in and about doing your best in the midst of those circumstances.

Joseph's father loved him more than his other sons because he had been born to him in his old age. The biblical account tells us that the brothers "hated him and could not speak a kind word to him" (Gen. 38:4).

Joseph had a dream that he communicated to his brothers. In it they were all binding sheaves of grain, and Joseph said: "Suddenly my sheaf rose and stood upright, while your sheaves gathered around mine and bowed down to it." (Gen. 38:7). This caused Joseph's brothers to hate him all the more. And he had another dream: "This time the sun and moon and eleven stars were bowing down to me" (Gen. 38:9). What boldness! It infuriated Joseph's brothers. They would never bow down to their youngest brother!

Later, Joseph went to check on his brothers as they were tending their father's flocks: "but they saw him in the distance, and before he reached them, they plotted to kill him. Here comes that dreamer . . . let's kill him and throw him into one of these cisterns and say that a ferocious animal devoured him. Then we'll see what comes of his dreams" (Gen. 38:19-20).

Their plans, however, were thwarted. A caravan of Ishmaelites came by, and instead of killing Joseph, the brothers sold him as a slave to these men. They took him to Egypt, where he was sold to Potiphar, the captain of Pharaoh's guard. "The LORD was with Joseph and he prospered" (Gen. 39:2). Eventually, Potiphar put Joseph in charge of his household and everything he owned.

But trials came. Potiphar's wife falsely accused Joseph of adultery because he refused to go to bed with her. Potiphar, upon hearing the accusation, believed it, "burned with anger" (Gen. 39:19), and put Joseph in prison. Even in prison, however, God was with him: "He showed [Joseph] kindness and granted him favor in the eyes of the prison warden. So the warden put Joseph in charge of all those held in prison" (Gen. 39:21-22).

While in prison Joseph had plenty of time to feel forsaken and wonder about his life. Instead, he used that time to do what he could despite the situation he found himself in. Among other things, he interpreted the dreams of two of Pharaoh's officials who were also in the king's prison. Joseph asked one of them if, when he was released, he would mention him to Pharaoh. Later, upon release, that official forgot!

Two more years passed until Pharaoh himself had a dream, and the official remembered Joseph. He was called and interpreted the dream. Pharaoh was impressed with his wisdom and concluded: "You shall be in charge of my palace, and all my people are to submit to your orders. . . . I hereby put you in charge of the whole land of Egypt" (Gen. 41:40-41).

Soon there was a famine in the land as Joseph had predicted. His brothers came to Egypt to buy some grain. When Joseph's brother arrived "they bowed down to him with their faces to the ground" (Gen. 42:6)—just as in Joseph's dream about the sheaves. They didn't recognize him then, but later, when they did, they were terrified. Joseph reassured them by saying, "It was not you who sent me here, but God" (Gen. 45:8). That statement alone shows the incredible insights he had about his entire sojourn and captivity.

This story has so much in it—jealousy, revenge, stumbling blocks, testing of faith. Amazingly, Joseph was able to help others in the seemingly helpless situation he was in. Eventually, it became clear that everything was always under God's control, even when it appeared to be totally out of control. With that hindsight comes the heightened realization of how one man, Joseph, lived his life with incredible patience and faith. He also exhibited forgiveness toward those who meant to do him harm. Joseph understood that everything had a purpose, orchestrated by God. Had his brothers not sold him to the Ishmaelites, he would not have ended up as ruler in Egypt, nor would he have seen the fulfillment of God's plans for him.

Joseph could have tried to take over his life and resist what was happening to him in whatever way he could. He could have fought against his circumstances. Had he done so, he would have frustrated God's ultimate plan for him and no doubt messed things up.

It is easy to see how we, in following God's plan and path for our lives, have a challenge to trust Him when we find ourselves in circumstances we don't entirely understand. Do you believe that He is working in you to fulfill His purposes and that as you seek His will everything will work together for good?

Like Joseph you'll be tested. Later, however, you most likely will look back and say of your challenges, "God did mean it for good." Such testing then will usher you into the third stage, when you are busy helping others and not seeing the fruition of your dreams.

Dream Stage Three—What Is Happening to My Dream?

In the third stage, which is involvement with others while wondering where your dream is going, there is a tremendous temptation to doubt yourself or doubt the outcome of your dream. You have already read the stories of several women who faced such a challenge. This third stage provides a great opportunity to practice your dream. If you are helping people in your area of interest, you can start to learn what works and what doesn't. The feedback from others can be good, provided you listen and remain flexible. You can look on this time as an opportunity to finetune your efforts and to give of yourself.

I know a woman, Nancy, who wanted to make a career of singing and playing the piano. She spent untold hours practicing and taking lessons. And she made the rounds of several institutions where she thought she could launch her career. Nothing happened. While she waited, she decided to offer her talents freely, or at a minimum charge, wherever she could. More time passed until one day she did get the call she was waiting for. It was an opportunity to perform at a well-known hotel in New York. She decided to accept the offer, knowing too that this was probably the beginning for her.

Many times Nancy felt like giving up on her dream, but she reminded herself that she might never get a chance later in life to work on it with such diligence. Time restraints, getting older, having a family, moving away, could all prevent that. Nancy hung in there, and I'm sure that somewhere today she is adding joy to people's lives as they hear her sing and play.

All this makes me wonder—how many other women are quietly laboring in the trenches, giving of themselves while not giving up on their dream? At this moment I think of Kim and her story of wanting to be a filmmaker. I know that Kim has done many different things and worked at many jobs to keep her dream alive. I'm sure you know women in similar situations. Maybe you are there yourself.

Forgiving Others

It is my experience that before the fourth stage of a dream, when it becomes a reality, some serious things need to happen. I'm talking about handing your dream over to God to fulfill or not—letting go. This will mean you needn't fear you are using God for your own purposes. It also will mean that you aren't tied to a fixed outcome.

Something else may also be called for at this stage: forgiving anyone you feel may have wronged you. Check your attitude to make sure you aren't harboring ill will toward anyone. Lack of forgiveness is a real block and does more harm than good. It can also cause health problems.

In *First Things First,* on managing time and balancing life, Steven Covey, A. Roger Merrill, and Rebecca Merrill discuss the value of forgiveness.

> Principle-centered people are not into comparing, competing or criticizing. Others begin to feel they can depend on them to be honest, direct, and non-manipulative, to make and keep commitments, to walk their talk. Principle-centered people don't over-react to negative behaviors, criticism, or human weaknesses. They're quick to forgive. They don't carry grudges. They refuse to label, stereotype, categorize or pre-judge.[1]

Whether from a business, a personal, or a spiritual standpoint, these words make sense. And forgiving seventy times seven—total forgiveness—also makes sense.

The practice of forgiveness develops large hearts, not small hearts. Psychologists would tell us, though, that forgiving others does not mean suffering at the hands of others. If you feel you need help understanding that difference, I encourage you to seek advice from a professional. It's part of the process of getting unstuck in your life.

A Divided Heart

Another element that could prevent your dream from going forward is having last minute thoughts about the rightness of your dream for you. A person with a divided heart does not usually fulfill a dream. Of course, everyone has probing questions or concerns about a dream. A divided heart means you have *real* doubts that you are doing the right thing. If you feel this way, you would benefit from doing some of the reality checks we mentioned earlier. Being on the wrong path will not help you, and doubling your efforts to pursue that path will only build on that mistake.

Stage Four—A Dream Comes True

In the fourth stage, when you start to see your dreams coming true, that dream may literally explode on the scene. Could this account for all the "overnight successes"? Undoubtedly, these people have spent years working quietly in the trenches. We have all heard about movie stars who worked as waiters or waitresses while pursuing their dreams. Then, one day they are suddenly famous. A dream often comes to fruition just when the dreamer has about given up on it. You have heard the expression, "It is darkest right before the dawn."

I can remember years ago when my husband and I started our label company. We were young and believed very much in what we were doing, but we were about to exhaust the resources that launched the company. By our calculations we were one month away from seeing our dream-business collapse. That month was the month the business took off—not by leaps and bounds—but it definitely turned the corner. That was a pretty close call. We would be tested again in the years to come, but we were on our way.

It will be exciting and rewarding when you start to see your own dream come true. With that will come increased awareness that your plans and goals are part of an even larger plan, designed for the benefit of others, not just for you alone. Being in tune with God's plan will keep you from envying others and their accomplishments.

Some would say to have a dream is to be selfish, only thinking of yourself. In reality pursuing a dream may require you to give of yourself in new and bolder ways to those you would seek to help or serve. Baroness Caroline's story in chapter four certainly illustrates this point.

I spoke with a friend recently who is pursuing

her dream and helping others. The dream pieces seem to be fitting together, but she needs financial provision to keep it going. She voiced her concern to me: "I have had to go back to God and say, 'If this is your service dream for me, then help my dream to be able to sustain itself.'"

I could tell that my friend was looking for answers and guidance. I asked her one important question: "Do you feel you are on the right path and are trusting God?" She answered with an unequivocal, "Yes!" I told her she had her answer. She could leave the outcome and timing to God. She had to trust that the financial piece of her dream would come into place one way or another. It would take time and patience. (Remember Bina's story earlier in this chapter?) God is aware of my friend's circumstances.

God's Word tells us: "God is able to make all grace abound to you, so that in all things at all times, having all that you need, you will abound in every good work" (2 Cor. 9:8). Notice the number of times *all* is used in that verse! God's provision for you may come from a variety of places—people, circumstances, or events. As you give your time, your talents, and your money for God's purposes, things will come together in amazing ways.

You can learn so much as you pursue your dream's journey, with all of its different stages. First, you'll feel that initial excitement as ideas flow into you. One of them will capture your interest in a unique way. Second, your dream idea will be tested. This will include a time of waiting and the testing of your mettle. Third, you will come to the stage where you are helping others and still not seeing your own dream blossom. Finally, you will see your dream come into being.

As you read the following two stories, you will notice the various stages of a dream unfolding. May they encourage you to follow your heart, forging ahead to see your dream come true.

Cheryl—director of corporate and foundation relations/development

Cheryl is a capable person who, in following her heart, has done a variety of things. And her journey is ongoing, including a recent change in her life. She sees herself as "an evolving person in process." You'll see how she has allowed that process to happen and where it has led her.

"I looked back recently over the little things I've done in my life and decided it is a bit like mountain climbing. I have a different point of view or vantage point, depending on where I am. I make different choices based on experience levels or exposure. I have a tendency to define myself in two ways: work I have done and relationships I have had. I think of myself as an evolving person, and right now I'm in mid-life process. I'm grateful for all I have done over the years because each piece is a building block. Nothing is wasted in God's economy.

"At age thirty, God took my life apart and put it back together the way He would have it to be when I decided to trust Him with my life. Several years later I found myself as a single parent with two children and a full-time sales job, based on commission. I had to learn to stand on my own two feet emotionally.

"When I went to college, I thought I'd be a teacher, get married, and be taken care of. It would be like Ozzie and Harriet—a house in the suburbs with a white picket fence, three kids, and a dog. After college, while married, I began teaching in North Carolina. I enjoyed the students and subject matter—French—but I didn't want to do that for the rest of my life.

"I moved away from teaching into something I loved, which was art and interior design. I walked into a shop I really liked and said, 'I'll do anything. Do you have a spot for me? I don't have any training.' The woman hired me as an apprentice. I was making less money, but I loved what I was doing. For three years I had a great time. I worked in interior design and as a designer and a buyer. I truly enjoyed working with colors and textures. But I became intrigued with the sales reps. They were men. They covered multiple states as representatives for textile houses. I thought this was what I wanted to do—selling in a broader setting with travel.

"I moved to Connecticut and went to an

employment agency. I said I wanted to get into sales. The agency sent me for an interview to a contract furniture dealership, and I was hired on the spot. After training I was sent out to talk to corporations. One year later I moved again because of my husband's job and went to a similar company on Long Island. (It was later in 1984 that I was to become a single parent for four-and-a-half years.)

"In the contract furniture business I met and married my instructor. I was selling Fortune 500 companies furniture by the hundreds and had many major accounts. I spent eight years in that industry until it became dry and purposeless for me. Selling five thousand mauve chairs to Barclays Bank just didn't seem to matter anymore. Even though I was making very good money, the job was no longer satisfying. I didn't really know what to do. I did not want to go back to teaching or to interior design. I wanted to use my business skills more directly and for more meaningful purposes.

"I took a course sponsored by Career Impact Ministries. I learned that in the field of development I would still be in sales, but with organizations that line up with my personal faith and beliefs. I wanted to make a difference. So over the next two years, I learned all I could about development work in a nonprofit setting.

"I thought about who could help me find out what development is—someone in the field itself.

(I'm a firm believer in picking other people's brains.) I went to a consultant who places development people. He said he couldn't help me because I had no experience, but he suggested I volunteer to do something related to development and get to know more.

"I was still working in New York, but I was home every Friday. I decided to use that time to do volunteer work and do another apprenticeship. I also did a lot of research and talking with people— people who were in the position or place I'd like to be. . . . I found people to be very gracious and helpful. I called the director of a local development department at a private Christian school and told him, 'I'd like to volunteer for some time on Fridays.' We talked and laid out a course of what I would do. One week later I was offered a job in development at the school.

"I have discovered I love the process of development. I love raising money for a worthy organization. I am 'selling' the school to donors and that matters. The product I have makes a difference in young lives, who can then go out and make our world better. I've discovered the world of Christian nonprofits, and I have learned a lot. I have seen people who *are* making the world better. This is a perfect synthesis of my business skills, my faith, and my teaching skills.

"I'd like to get my master's either in business

or nonprofit management. I would like a broader sphere, with bigger geography, bigger numbers, and more responsibility.

"There are always challenges, such as the fear of change, the fear of success, or fear of failure. I have found it helpful to keep a journal. I write everything down. I ask myself, 'What are you afraid of?' Then I write down the answer. When I look at that fear in the light of day, solutions come. I also ask myself, 'What is the worst that can happen—what is the best?' The process of really confronting fears and writing about them helps me think through things. I visualize the way things could go, positively or negatively. . . . Then I do my homework and ACT.

"I think women should learn to trust their instincts, move forward, and not be fearful of making mistakes. Very few are irreparable. With God's help, and because of the gifts He has given us, we can shape our tomorrows by the choices we make today."

Cheryl is someone who, with God's help, has shaped her tomorrows. She also has been very proactive in taking action steps toward her goals (which may give you some ideas of your own). She is now Regional Director of Advancement for Charles Colson's Prison Fellowship, working in the Western Central states, the Mid-Atlantic states, and Washington, DC. She works with major donors and does some consulting. I asked Cheryl how she enjoys her new vocation: "I am energized by seeing how God is working in all corners of the world, and by having an opportunity to articulate a vision of ministry to so many people. . . . I love what I am doing."

Grace—caregiver, home for drug rehabilitation

God's hand in Grace's life was evident as He went before her, preparing the way while she followed in faith. At first, she kept saying other people should do the things she had on her heart, and she would pray for them. Then one day she realized that those passions were meant for her. They were God's calling.

"I was raised in a Christian home. My dad was pastor of an Italian church in Newton, Massachusetts. My life was very affected by my parents. My mom had compassion and love for people. My father brought faith into the home. As a child, in the morning I would sneak around the corner to see what he was doing, and there he would be on his knees praying. I remember saying to myself, 'Whatever he has, I want.'

"I dedicated my life to the Lord at age twelve and said to God, 'I'll do what you want me to do.' I didn't know what the future would hold. I always thought I'd be an elementary school teacher. The last year of high school something changed my direction. I attended a special service where young men from a Christian rehabilitation center shared their personal stories. One by one they told of bondage to drugs and alcohol and how they were set free by the power of Christ.

"That night I couldn't sleep. I kept thinking about the rehabilitation work I had been exposed to. I felt I was being drawn to that work. What could I possibly do—I was only seventeen years old and had just graduated from high school? I had never been on drugs or smoked, and because I had an Italian father, would probably never leave home until I was married!

"In my persistence and with God's help, I convinced my dad to allow me to go down to the rehabilitation ministry and find out if there was anything I could do. I will never forget going down to the ministry, knocking on the door, and having the director greet me by saying, 'We just began a work for women. We have a director for the program, but no one to work with her.' Two weeks later I was living and working in an environment I didn't know existed. There were women from all walks of life at the center—prostitutes, drug users, women coming out of prison. All of them were older than me and very streetwise. I remember them saying, 'You are just a kid. What can you tell us?'

"I would cry to the Lord, 'Why did You bring me to this place? What can I possibly give these women? I haven't been on the streets. I don't understand their pain or speak their language.'

"The Lord spoke to my heart and said, 'What have I given you? Haven't I given you my love and my Word? This is what you are to share.' I felt like Abraham going to the land I knew nothing of—a place where I had left family, friends, and security, only to obey and follow God's direction.

"Needless to say, my year at the center was a time of growing up and maturing in my dependence on God. It was there I met George, who later became my husband. (He was working on the staff as a counselor to men.) I grew to love George as I saw the heart he had for God. Many times I told him, 'You were born just for me.'

"George and I both went on to school. I left after two years to save money for our wedding. Meanwhile I applied for a job at a bank and spent five years there, even though I hadn't planned on it. (God says the steps of a good man are ordered by the Lord!)

"At the bank I met many people who would later help with my future work. At that time George was working for the state of Massachusetts and volunteering time at a prison. A young man asked him about finding a Christian home for his wife who was on drugs. To our amazement we could not find one Christian home for women dealing with substance abuse problems. We did the Christian thing and prayed that someone would begin a work for women! We prayed and sought counsel for two years until God said, 'I want you to do it.'

"Here was our dream, and we prayed that God would help us. We traveled, sharing our vision with churches. Many people would say, 'Come back to us when you have your home.' At the same time calls came from people asking, 'Do you have a place yet? My daughter is on the street,' or 'my sister is in desperate need.'

"We looked at potential homes that could house a women's work. We wanted something in a country atmosphere away from the drug scene. We looked at many properties, including mansions, even though we might have had sixteen cents in our pockets. We would see a property we wanted, but we would wonder, 'How, Lord?' I became tired of looking. What should I do?

"I had been working and talking about my burdens with people and nothing was happening. I felt I had to launch out into the deep. Like Peter and John fishing, I had caught nothing. Nevertheless, I would let down my nets. I remember one day I was weeping and saying to God, 'Show us the way.' Then I saw an ad in the paper for a home on thirty-two acres of land—to lease with an option to buy. We went to look at it and the Lord said to me, 'This is the home.' I knew He had put this in my heart. But as we walked into the house, things were so bad I could hardly stand it. However, I knew God had spoken and I saw the potential.

"We went back to the realtor, and he said to have $1,500 dollars by Monday morning. We didn't know where the money was coming from. God miraculously supplied. A well-known Christian businessman, whom I had met though Chuck Colson's mother when I was working at the bank, gave us $1,000. George then spoke at a small church that weekend and the secretary of the church told us she wanted to give us $500 as part of her tithe. Would that be okay?

"We had our first home for women. Two-and-a-half years later we sold it because we had already outgrown it, We moved to a beautiful home in Manchester, New Hampshire. New Life Home for Women has been there for seventeen years, helping women with drug and alcohol related problems. We take in women who are single and women with children. (Having the children with her helps a mother complete a program if she doesn't have anywhere to place them.) We provide for the needs of both mother and child. And we take in unwed pregnant young ladies. By the time women reach us, they have such low self-esteem and are hopeless. They need supportive counseling.

"God gave me a heart for women—His heart and His eyes. He has helped me overlook the hardness but feel their pain and see through the eyes of faith what they can become. It has long been in my heart to touch lives. I want others to experience what I have experienced and to know God's love. My prayer is that people will hear my story and grow in faith.

"This has been a work of faith, with many tests and challenges, but God has been faithful. People don't realize many times that the dreams and visions they have within themselves are placed there by the Lord. To other women I would say, 'Be persistent in faith and in prayer and believe that God will direct your steps.'"

When I review Grace's story, it is clear that God directed her steps and that He is carrying out the purposes He has for her life and the women she serves. I hope that her story helped you grow in faith, realizing what God can do as you trust Him and as He leads the way. Grace has other dreams too—she has talked of writing a book to document all that has happened and how God has blessed her and those whose lives she has been privileged to touch at New Life.

Sharing Your Dream-Journey

By now you've seen there will be some obstacles and even struggles, along with joys, as you strive to create the future you desire. No matter how challenging your own life and circumstances are, however, you can make a decision to do something about those circumstances and about your dreams. It will ultimately be your decisions, and not your circumstances, that will most affect your destiny.

Fellow dreamers such as Cheryl and Grace are each taking a unique journey, but they no doubt have many of the same hopes you do—to excel in the work and dreams God has given to them. Look for these fellow travelers and cheer them on as they do the same for you. Together, you will create a rich legacy as you offer God and others the best of your talents and service.

It is important in the early stages of your dream not only to believe in yourself, but also to surround yourself with a support system. At the start of this book, I mentioned possibly having several interested friends into your home to go through some of the exercises in this book, as you each share your dream-journeys and goals in an atmosphere of mutual desire and trust. If you choose not to do this, you could share your dreams and plans with one or two trusted friends who will encourage you *and* tell you if they think you are not thinking clearly.

You may have a spouse as a support system. Be aware that your spouse may need time to understand what you want to do or to understand why you want to do it.

I believe that when you seek God's will for your life, rather than saying, "I'm going to do this thing I want, regardless" your husband will see that your priorities are right. Then he can help you use your abilities in ways that are pleasing to God.

My husband, Len, has been an incredible support to me. He has encouraged me when I needed encouraging, given me ideas when I seemed to be stymied, prayed for me as I waited for my dreams to materialize, and generally been my cheering section. He senses that what I am doing seems to be God's timing and purpose for my life. Each victory, no matter how small, becomes something we celebrate together and thank God for. As we see God's hand at work, we grow together in our faith. I am very grateful for such a caring, helpful partner in my dream pursuits.

When you are seeking the support of others in the pursuit of your dream, remember that garnering ideas, making contacts, and seeking advice and know-how can all help you present your dream as a stable undertaking. You may want to do some background work before you tell anyone. Later, when you do present your ideas, your legwork will demonstrate to others that you have put time into your dream and are not following a sudden whim. This makes it more real.

A Fraternity of Dreamers

It has been a privilege to have many women share their dreams with me—and with you. Dreams are very personal to each of us. Revealing a dream is like revealing your innermost thoughts. By letting others hear these thoughts, you risk hearing either their approval or disapproval. You risk being vulnerable or giving up on your dream. Sometimes it all hangs in the balance somewhat delicately, and it doesn't take much to discourage your dream altogether. On the other hand those who dare to follow a dream and believe in it, will discover that there are others who do care and will offer all the love and support they can. These supporters form a fraternity with each other, much like the "fraternity" that mothers have with each other. These mothers are part of a club that has no dues and rejects no one. Upon meeting, whether on an airplane, in a cooking class, or at a social function, they trade stories of the joys and the trials they experience with their children. They go their own way with the knowledge and realization that they belong to a very special and blessed group of women.

Following a heart's quest is something we each have to do essentially on our own, but without God's help and the help of others we will never complete that quest. We dreamers also belong to a special fraternity as we give birth to ideas, ventures, and service opportunities that can not only provide great satisfaction, but also can enrich the lives of many. In doing so, we all are privileged.

The next chapter highlights promises from God that you can take with you on your dream's journey. It also discusses the truth that you never have to be alone in this adventure. There is One who wants to be with you all the way.

Chapter Nine

Promises to Keep You Going

If you have not yet taken proactive steps to test your dream for future possibilities, I assume you will be doing so in the upcoming days. The sooner you do this, the more tangible and real your dreams will become.

Throughout this book we have discussed two main points. First, as you follow your heart to discover the dreams God has placed within you, you will find others taking that same journey; you are not alone. Second, in the course of pursuing your dream, you will be led on a heart's journey that may take you into uncharted waters or unfamiliar terrain, with some risk involved.

How can you prepare for that uncertainty, or can

you prepare for it? I believe that the care and prayer you have been putting into this endeavor will help you greatly. I also believe something else can undergird your journey. I am speaking of God and His promises, which serve as a road map for those times of risk or uncertainty. I have highlighted these promises throughout the book, but they deserve an even closer look.

God is not somebody far away who may or may not be interested in your affairs; rather He is someone who wants an intimate relationship with you because He cares for you deeply: "And even the very hairs of your head are all numbered. . . . You are worth more than many sparrows" (Matt. 10:30-31). God is also someone who thinks about you a lot: "How precious to me are your thoughts, O God! How vast is the sum of them! Were I to count them, they would outnumber the grains of sand" (Ps. 139:17-18).

While many of us acknowledge a personal faith in God, we often live our lives independent of any trusting relationship with Him, carrying our own burdens, making our own decisions, worrying about a million things daily. We do this despite His promise: "Come to me, all you who are weary and burdened, and I will give you rest. . . . For my yoke is easy and my burden is light" (Matt. 11:28-30). The yoke we put on ourselves is the difficult one. It indicates that we either don't trust God enough to give our dreams and our lives completely to Him, or we simply can't relinquish control over our plans and goals. So we miss out on God's richest blessings and on developing our faith. Pursuing a dream is a good time to discover not only your own desires, but also to develop an even closer relationship with God.

When you see God at work in your life, often working things out in ways you never could, do you wonder why you didn't give Him full control sooner? Perhaps such a situation fills you with new resolve to put Him first in everything if you haven't always done that. Your life will take on new meaning as you learn to have faith in God.

It is exciting that you are daring to do new things and pursuing your God-given dream. Maybe you are someone who has not had a personal relationship with God, or maybe you just go to God for the BIG things. Don't be afraid to seek closeness with Him. God longs for you to invite Him into your life: "Here I am! I stand at the door and knock. If anyone hears my voice and opens the door, I will come in and eat with him, and he with me" (Rev. 3:20). When you invite Christ to live within you, He gives you His Spirit to guide you: "I will instruct you and teach you in the way you should go; I will counsel you and watch over you" (Ps. 32:8).

It is easy for any of us not to fully grasp all the good things God has in store for us: "I have come that they may have life, and have it to the full" (John 10:10). Do you believe that? Do you have that kind of life? Do you know other biblical promises about life, living, faith, gifts/talents, work, or happiness and success? These promises will help you as you pursue your dream, but they will also help you with the stress, struggle, excitement, and joy of daily life.

Years ago I heard Norman Vincent Peale speak in the Marble Collegiate Church in New York City. He talked about God's biblical truth principles (promises). He said that he was going to mention some and that we could put them in a box (mentally) and take them home with us. We could then go to the box, lift the lid, so to speak, and take out the promises when we needed to apply them to a particular challenge or situation. Or, we could let the box sit on a shelf, gathering dust in the recesses of our heart and mind.

I have never forgotten Dr. Peale's advice. And so, here are some promises that you can store away in your own "box." Whenever you need support, direction, or encouragement, lift the lid and pull out a promise. The list does not include all of the "great and precious promises" God has given us, but it does include truths that apply to anyone who is looking for direction and guidance. These promises consider the three questions we referred to at the start of this book: *Who am I? Where do I want to go? How can I get there?*

Promises and Truth Principles
Desires

"May he give you the desires of your heart and make

all your plans succeed" (Ps. 20:4).

"Delight yourself also in the LORD and he will give you the desires of your heart" (Ps. 37:4).

"Hope deferred makes the heart sick, but a longing fulfilled is a tree of life" (Prov. 13:12).

"If you remain in me and my words remain in you, ask whatever you wish, and it will be given you" (John 15:7).

Gifts/Talents

"We have different gifts, according to the grace given us" (Rom. 12:6).

"For we are God's workmanship, created in Christ Jesus to do good works, which God prepared in advance for us to do" (Eph. 2:10).

"It is God who works in you to will and to act according to His good purpose" (Phil. 2:13).

"Each one should use whatever gift he has received to serve others, faithfully administering God's grace in its various forms" (1 Peter 4:10).

Path/Guidance

"I will instruct you and teach you in the way you should go; I will counsel you and watch over you" (Ps. 32:8).

"Trust in the LORD with all your heart and lean not on your own understanding; in all your ways acknowledge him, and he will make your paths straight" (Prov. 3:5-6).

"Whether you turn to the right or to the left, your ears will hear a voice behind you, saying, 'This is the way; walk in it'" (Isa. 30:21).

"I am the LORD your God, who teaches you what is best for you, who directs you in the way you should go" (Isa. 48:17).

Faith

"I tell you the truth, if you have faith as small as a mustard seed, you can say to this mountain, 'Move from here to there,' and it will move. Nothing will be impossible for you" (Matt. 17:20).

"If you believe, you will receive whatever you ask for in prayer" (Matt. 21:22).

"So I say to you: Ask and it will be given to you; seek and you will find; knock and the door will be opened to you. For everyone who asks receives; he who seeks finds; and to him who knocks, the door will be opened" (Luke 11:9-10).

"Now faith is being sure of what we hope for and certain of what we do not see " (Heb. 11:1).

Work

"She considers a field and buys it; out of her earnings she plants a vineyard. She sets about her work vigorously; her arms are strong for her tasks. . . . Give her the reward she has earned, and let her works bring her praise at the city gate" (Prov. 31:16-17, 31).

"I am the vine; you are the branches. If a man remains in me and I in him, he will bear much fruit; apart from me you can do nothing. . . . You did not choose me, but I chose you and appointed you to go and bear fruit—fruit that will last" (John 15:5,16).

"For we are God's workmanship, created in Christ Jesus to do good works, which God prepared in advance for us to do" (Eph. 2:10).

"And we pray this in order that you may live a life worthy of the Lord and may please Him in every way: bearing fruit in every good work, growing in the knowledge of God . . ." (Col. 1:10).

Plans

"May he give you the desires of your heart and make all your plans succeed" (Ps. 20:4).

"Plans fail for lack of counsel, but with many advisers they succeed" (Prov. 15:22).

"Commit to the LORD whatever you do, and your plans will succeed" (Prov. 16:3).

"'For I know the plans I have for you,' declares the LORD, . . . 'plans to give you hope and a future'" (Jer. 29:11).

Joy/Abundance

"I have told you this so that my joy may be in you and that your joy may be complete" (John 15:11).

"Until now you have not asked for anything in my name. Ask and you will receive, and your joy will be complete" (John 16:24).

"No eye has seen, nor ear has heard, no mind has conceived what God has prepared for those who love Him" (1 Cor. 2:9).

"Now to him who is able to do immeasurably more than all we ask or imagine, according to his power that is at work within us" (Eph. 3:20).

Some of these truths, as you appropriate them within your heart, may be what will keep you going as you move in the direction of your dream, stepping out in faith even though you do not yet see the fulfillment of that dream. This can be especially true when you have laid the groundwork but nothing seems to be happening (stage three). It was during such times in my own journey that I was driven to these promises of God. I decided to test them myself to determine whether there was any truth in them, or if they were just warm, fuzzy statements. Could they really offer hope? Or were they merely empty promises? Even though these promises don't represent a covenant God has with us, they do represent His wisdom and desire for our lives. And they often require things of us.

I have found that God's promises are indeed true. In fact, they are as true and as operative as the law of gravity.

I encourage you to do four things as you consider the promises included in this chapter. If you follow these steps, I believe you will experience the reality of the truths conveyed.

1. Assume each promise means exactly what it says. Don't try to interpret it or add to it or read between the lines.

2. Prepare your heart and mind to believe the promises, with the belief that God can be trusted, that He loves you, and that He wants only the best for you.

3. If part of the promise depends on your action, be willing to take that step. Some promises state what God will do and what you should do. Others are statements of truth. Consider Proverbs 3:5: "Trust in the Lord with all your heart and lean not on your own understanding; in all your ways acknowledge Him . . ." This verse, for example, tells you to trust God wholeheartedly, not to put full trust in your own understanding, and to acknowledge God in "all your ways." (That means you should see God's hand in every detail or effort in your life, no detail being too small.) If you do this, what will God do? "He will make your paths straight," or as some translations say, "He shall direct thy paths" (KJV).

4. After you have done these three things, be willing to wait for God's timing and be willing to let go of your control over your dream.

By the way, if you have a hard time believing some of these truths, tell God you "will" yourself to believe them. Your will has more power than your feelings. Say to God, "I do believe; help me overcome my unbelief!" (Mark 9:24) Would any of us ever think we had enough faith to qualify for God's blessing or guidance if it depended on how much we could muster? Maybe that is why Christ told us we just needed faith the size of a mustard seed. (Have you ever seen a mustard seed?)

God sometimes allows trials and suffering to accompany the many promises He has given to us. When we experience those times, we can trust Him even though we may not like or understand what we are going through. Things do work together for good, especially as we surrender hard times or circumstances beyond our control to God. A hindsight perspective reveals this to be true; however, we may never have all the answers we want in this life. We can simply pray and seek God's best. We are told "suffering produces perseverance; perseverance, character; and character, hope. And hope does not disappoint us . . ." (Rom. 5:3-5). God's ways and thoughts are higher than our own.

I have written this book from my own experiences and faith, but I have a sensitivity to any readers who may be searching for a stronger faith or answers for their own lives. I echo the words Richard Nelson Bolles stated in his book *What Color is Your Parachute?* Like Mr. Bolles, I count on others to translate my thoughts/beliefs into their own, trying them out for themselves. As Bolles stated, "This ability to thus translate is the indispensable sine qua non of anyone who aspires to communicate helpfully with others."[1]

In conclusion, I believe, as does Bolles, that our mission in life is a law "written in our members." In other words, God has already revealed His will for you, relating to your vocation and mission. You discern this by looking at your talents and skills, especially those you most delight to use—the very topics we have covered in this book.

You have undoubtedly learned much about yourself by now and begun to experience the faith walk of your dream-journey. That will begin to change how you look at your life and how you give of yourself. It is my desire that in the days ahead you will have the union of heart, mind, and spirit that will enable you to follow your heart and find your dreams. May you continue to believe that God will help you fulfill the dream He has given you. As you do, your life will be made richer and the world will only benefit.

I would love to hear about your dream. Are you in the waiting process, or have you begun to see the fulfillment of your dream? Write to me at the following address or contact me for speaking engegements concerning following your heart.

Judy Peterson
P. O. Box 1155
Wilton, NH 03086

Endnotes

Chapter 1

1 Donna K. H. Walters, "Women: The New Providers," *Los Angeles Times,* May 11, 1995, part A, page 1.

2 Nanci Hellmich, "Down-home Jan Karon author's religious 'Song,'" *USA Today*, April 14, 1999, D-2.

3 Ibid.

4 Ibid.

5 Hannah Whitall Smith, *The Christian's Secret of a Happy Life* (New Jersey: Fleming H. Revell Co, MCMLII), 98.

6 Ibid., 99.

Chapter 2

1 Arthur F. Miller and Ralph T. Mattson, *The Truth About You* (Berkeley, California: Ten Speed Press, 1989), 4.

2 Ibid., 40.

3 Gail Sheehy, *New Passages* (New York: Random House, 1995), 153.

4 Ibid.

5 Mary Beth Franklin, "Heaven Can't Wait," *Chicago Tribune,* September 17, 1995, 13-3.

6 Ibid.

7 Ibid.

Chapter 3

1 Arthur F. Miller and Ralph T. Mattson, *The Truth about You,* 50.

Chapter 4:

1 Patricia Aburdene and John Naisbitt, *Megatrends for Women* (New York: Villard Books, 1992), 64.

2 Ibid.

3 Gary Crooker, "These Women Are Just 'Mad' About Their Business," *The Milford N.H. Cabinet and Wilton Journal,* May 17, 1995, 13.

4 Ibid.

Chapter 5

1 Henry David Thoreau, *Walden* (New York: Bramhall House, MCMLI), 343.

2 Anthony Robbins, *Awaken the Giant Within* (New York: Fireside, 1991), 304.

3 Abraham H. Maslow, *Toward a Psychology of Being* (New York: Van Nostrand Company, 1968), 47.

Chapter 6

1 Viktor Frankl, *Man's Search for Meaning* (New York: Pocket Books, 1959), 164.

Chapter 7

1 Zan Dubin, "Slimmed Down and Coming Back for Seconds," *Los Angeles Times,* May 6, 1995, F-2.

2 Judith Gaines, "Growing Number of Elderly off Their Rocker and Loving It," *Boston Globe*, October 2, 1994, Metro/region, 1.

Chapter 8

1 Stephen R. Covey, A. Roger Merrill, Rebecca R. Merrill, *First Things First* (New York: Simon and Schuster, 1994), 292.

Chapter 9

1 Richard Nelson Bolles, *What Color Is Your Parachute?* (New York: Ten Speed Press, 1994), 432.

Suggested Reading

Drake, Marsha. *The Proverbs 31 Lady and Other Impossible Dreams*. Minneapolis: Bethany House Publishing, 1984.

Gire, Ken. *The Reflective Life*. Colorado Springs: Chariot Victor Publishing, 1998.

Littauer, Florence. *Taking Charge of Your Life*. Grand Rapids: Revell, 1999.

Macy, Howard R. *Rhythms of the Inner Life*. Colorado Springs: Chariot Victor Publishing, 1999.

Meyer, Joyce. *How to Succeed at Being Yourself*. Tulsa: Harrison House, 1999.

Miller, Arthur F. with William Hendricks. *Why You Can't Be Anything You Want to Be*. Grand Rapids: Zondervan Publishing House, 1999.

Noble, Diane. *It's Time: Explore Your Dreams and Discover Your Gifts (For Me)*. Grand Rapids: Baker Book House, 1995.

Smith, Hannah Whitall. *The Christian's Secret of a Happy Life*. Westwood, NJ: Flemming H. Revell Co., 1952.

Swindoll, Charles. *The Mystery of God's Will*. Nashville: Word Publishing, 1999.

A Personal Note
From the
Author

Heart

Trust, lean not on ourselves, acknowledge God; we are instructed to do these things and God will direct our paths. They sound easy, but it is a constant challenge to entrust our dreams to God. We worry or wonder whether our dreams will really ever get off the ground. When they do, we still can't quite let go and let God take over. It is my hope you will look upon your dream as God at work in you "to will and to act according to his good purpose" (Phil. 2:13).

Soul

Trust in the Lord with all your heart
and lean not on your own understanding;
in all your ways acknowledge him,
and he will make your paths straight.
Proverbs 3:5-6

Mind

I heartily recommend any book by Hannah Whitall Smith, author of the classic *The Christian's Secret of a Happy Life*, first published in 1870! Hannah Smith grasped the truth principles of the Bible. Her writing appeals to anyone who has an incredible urge to know God's secrets and promises, and how to find and walk the higher hidden road.

Strength

 Believe that God has given you your deepest desires to fulfill His purposes for your life. As those desires grow, take one step at a time even when you aren't sure where it is all lead ing. Trust that a path will emerge. Then have faith in following it. This will require quiet times of reflec-tion and prayer, as important a discipline as goal setting and action plans. Make such times a part of every week. They will help you stay the course.

I pray that each reader of this book will experience fulfillment of her dreams as she learns to trust the Giver of those dreams.

Judy Peterson